FORTRESS • 80

BRITISH FORTS IN THE AGE OF ARTHUR

ANGUS KONSTAM   ILLUSTRATED BY PETER DENNIS

Series editors Marcus Cowper and Nikolai Bogdanovic

First published in 2008 by Osprey Publishing
Midland House, West Way, Botley, Oxford OX2 0PH, UK
44-02 23rd St, Suite 219, Long Island City, NY 11101, USA
Email: info@ospreypublishing.com

© 2008 Osprey Publishing Limited

All rights reserved. Apart from any fair dealing for the purpose of private
study, research, criticism or review, as permitted under the Copyright,
Designs and Patents Act, 1988, no part of this publication may be
reproduced, stored in a retrieval system, or transmitted in any form
or by any means, electronic, electrical, chemical, mechanical, optical,
photocopying, recording or otherwise, without the prior written
permission of the copyright owner. Enquiries should be addressed
to the Publishers.

ISBN: 978 1 84603 362 9

Page layout by Ken Vail Graphic Design, Cambridge, UK (kvgd.com)
Cartography: Map Studio, Romsey, UK
Index by Sandra Shotter
Originated by PDQ Digital Media Solutions
Printed in China through Bookbuilders

10 11 12 13 14   11 10 9 8 7 6 5 4 3 2

A CIP catalogue record for this book is available from the British Library.

FOR A CATALOGUE OF ALL BOOKS PUBLISHED BY OSPREY
MILITARY AND AVIATION PLEASE CONTACT:

Osprey Direct, c/o Random House Distribution Center,
400 Hahn Road, Westminster, MD 21157
Email: uscustomerservice@ospreypublishing.com

Osprey Direct, The Book Service Ltd, Distribution Centre,
Colchester Road, Frating Green, Colchester, Essex, CO7 7DW
Email: customerservice@ospreypublishing.com

www.ospreypublishing.com

ARTIST'S NOTE

Readers may care to note that the original paintings from which the
colour plates in this book were prepared are available for private sale.
All reproduction copyright whatsoever is retained by the Publishers.
All enquiries should be addressed to:

Peter Dennis, Fieldhead, The Park, Mansfield, Nottinghamshire
NG18 2AT, UK

The Publishers regret that they can enter into no correspondence upon
this matter.

THE FORTRESS STUDY GROUP (FSG)

The object of the FSG is to advance the education of the public in the
study of all aspects of fortifications and their armaments, especially
works constructed to mount or resist artillery. The FSG holds an annual
conference in September over a long weekend with visits and evening
lectures, an annual tour abroad lasting about eight days, and an annual
Members' Day.

The FSG journal FORT is published annually, and its newsletter Casemate
is published three times a year. Membership is international. For further
details, please contact:

The Secretary, c/o 6 Lanark Place, London W9 1BS, UK

Website: www.fsgfort.com

THE WOODLAND TRUST

Osprey Publishing are supporting the Woodland Trust, the UK's leading
woodland conservation charity, by funding the dedication of trees.

CONTENTS

THE FORTIFICATIONS OF BRITAIN IN THE AGE OF ARTHUR

INTRODUCTION

This book covers the period from the departure of the Romans from Britain at the start of the 5th century AD until AD 600, a convenient point to mark the consolidation of the Anglo-Saxon kingdom across most of modern England. Whether you believe King Arthur to be a historical character, a semi-mythical figure or even an invention of medieval romantics, he is closely identified with this period – one of the most formative periods in the historical development of the British Isles. The archaeologist Leslie Alcock first coined the phrase 'Arthur's Britain' in 1971, offering legitimacy to the populist association between Arthur and the period. Two years later the historian John Morris published *The Age of Arthur*, reinforcing the association even further.

Since then the historical debate over Arthur's identity, his role and his very existence has raged fiercely, and today historians are just about as divided on the issue as they were almost four decades ago. Morris has largely been discredited, but his views still remain popular with those who simply want to believe in Arthur as a historical figure. Recently his views have been reappraised by a new generation of historians – both academic and amateur – and the battle over Arthur's existence is now hotly debated once more.

The problem is largely one of historical sources – or more accurately the lack of them. Our main source is the Celtic monk Gildas, whose *De Excidio et Conquestu Britanniae* (*On the Ruin and Conquest of Britain*) was probably written in the mid 6th century AD. His book was a sermon – a rallying cry to the people of Britain – but it also contained a brief summary of the recent history of Britain. He made no mention of Arthur, an omission

The 25ft (8m)-deep ditch which lay on the southern side of the Devil's Dyke was substantial, presenting a significant obstacle to an attacker. Thus of all the dykes in East Anglia this one could have been used as a military barrier as well as being a territorial boundary.
(Sam Marks)

which has fuelled the anti-Arthurian argument, but which in itself is probably not entirely conclusive. Gildas probably wrote it around AD 550, which places him at the height of the conflict between Briton and Saxon. His writing is augmented by other British authors (Nennius' *Historia Brittonum* or the *Annales Cambriae*), later Anglo-Saxon sources (*The Anglo-Saxon Chronicle* or Bede's *Ecclesiastical History*), or by works written abroad, such as Constantius' *Life of Germanus of Auxerre*. The trouble with these is that hard historical facts are sparse, and the sources are often contradictory.

Fortunately there is also a growing caucus of archaeological evidence, and while the Arthurian debate was going on archaeologists were revealing fresh information about the end of Roman rule in Britain, and what happened in the two centuries which followed. Towards the end of the 4th century AD Roman towns in Britain appear to have undergone a noticeable decline in population, becoming little more than marketplaces. At the same time there are signs of increased rural activity, centred on the Roman villas whose agricultural production continued to remain high.

By the time the Roman army departed from Britain around AD 409 the province they left behind was reasonably prosperous, but undergoing major changes. The biggest of these was the collapse of central administration, which until then had been based in Londinium (London). Britannia was divided into four smaller provinces, which were in turn divided into *civitates* (the equivalent of counties). Government still appeared to function at this

Tintagel is a fortification of Late Antiquity that took full advantage of its geographical position. The 'Arthurian' fort occupied a similar location to the medieval structure seen here. A main defensive perimeter was located on the mainland, while the island contained clusters of religious and secular buildings. (RCAM)

Fortresses of the Saxon Shore – a medieval copy of a lost 10th-century map. The nine forts shown are Bradwell, Dover, Lymphe, Brancaster, Burgh Castle, Reculver, Richborough, Pevensey and Portchester. (Bibliothèque Municipale, Rouen)

level, much as it had before. What had changed, though, was the collapse of the established monetary system, which included the collection and payment of taxes to maintain military garrisons and fleets. A barter system replaced coinage, while for the most part the regional *civitates* took over control of their own defences. While the money system broke down, law and order did not; the ruling post-Roman aristocracy of Britain continued to maintain their control over the province for the best part of a century after the legions were shipped over to Gaul.

However, Britannia was no longer protected by veteran legionaries. The great legionary fortresses lay abandoned, the Roman towns lacked proper defences, and the only troops available to defend the *civitates* from attack were whatever local troops could be raised to defend their own communities. This view has been challenged by those who believe the cleric Gildas, who claims that the provinces were united under a High King or 'Tyrant'. Unfortunately there is little hard evidence to support any such restoration of central authority in the 5th century AD. Instead it seems as if every region was left to its own devices. It was this lack of troops which – according to the *Anglo-Saxon Chronicle* – prompted the tyrant Vortigern to hire Saxon mercenaries as *foederati* (barbarian auxiliaries), thus inviting the wolf into the fold.

The long-accepted view of the coming of the Saxons was that in the late 5th century AD they rebelled against their post-Roman British paymasters, and promptly invited other waves of Angle and Saxon invaders to join them in a conquest of Britain. In recent years this view has been replaced by one of settlement rather than conquest, a gradual process which culminated in the late 5th century AD with the establishment of petty Anglo-Saxon kingdoms in the east and south-east of what is now England. These Saxons were once dismissed as barbarians, but archaeology has shown that they enjoyed a rich culture, and maintained trading links with the rest of Europe. The same is true of the Britons; pottery finds suggest a vibrant trade between south-west Britain and the continental mainland.

However, this was also a time of warfare. While many of the old Roman fortifications were abandoned, others were employed as defences against the Saxons. While recently archaeologists have suggested that the forts of the Saxon Shore were defended storehouses more than forts, references to their employment as bulwarks against the Saxons can be found in the *Anglo-Saxon Chronicle*. Similarly the archaeological evidence suggests that the post-Roman British also maintained fortified outposts on Hadrian's Wall, and probably in the old legionary fortresses farther to the south. It is also possible that some Roman towns – most notably Wroxeter in Shropshire – were used as military centres, or at least their defences were strengthened.

While this reoccupation of Roman defensive works helped provide some form of protection from Saxon, Pictish or Irish incursions, in many parts of Britain an even more suitable form of fortification was available. During the 5th and 6th centuries AD the long-abandoned Iron Age hill-forts which had

The late 3rd-century walls of the 'Saxon Shore' fort of Portis Adurni (Portchester) are still impressive, and probably represent one of the best surviving examples of late-Roman fortification. However, these forts remain something of an enigma, as there is little evidence of military activity within their walls during Late Antiquity. (Stratford Archive)

provided a brief rallying point against the Romans were pressed into service once more. In the south-west of Britain some of these old hill-forts were reoccupied, while in Wales a few new forts were built, designed to suit the needs of a new breed of British warlord. This book is the story of how all these forts developed during these crucial two centuries of British history.

The problem still remains, however, of what to call this period. In the past the phrase 'sub-Roman' was used, although 'post-Roman' is now more common. The phrase 'Dark Ages' has fallen from favour, as has the 'Barbarian Migration Era'. The phrase 'Pagan Saxon' has been used in reference to the early Saxon settlement of Britain, while 'late Celtic' or 'early Christian' also limit the period by linking it to one particular culture or faith. Lately the term 'Late Antiquity' has been suggested, as a means of promoting the idea that the legacy of Roman Britain survived the departure of the legions. In the popular imagination this is the period of Arthur – the time of Arthur's Britain.

CHRONOLOGY

Note: given the vagaries of dating in Late Antiquity, some of these dates are approximate, and may actually vary by a year or so either way.

AD 367	'The Barbarian Conspiracy': multiple attacks on Roman Britain.
383–88	Reign of Magnus Maximus, British contender for the imperial throne.
406	Vandals, Suevi and Alans cross the River Rhine and attack Roman Gaul.
409	Approximate date of departure of Roman army from Britain.
410	Sack of Rome by the Visigoths. Emperor Honorius tells Britons they must look to their own defences.
429	First visit to Britain by Germanus, Bishop of Auxerre.
c. 441	Date given in *Chronicles* for Saxon 'revolt'.
c. 450	According to Gildas, the Britons ask the Roman general Aetius for help. Bede dates the 'arrival of the English in Britain' to the same time.
482–511	Reign of Clovis, King of the Franks: Gaul is united under one ruler.
c. 500	Battle of Mount Badon: British victory leads to almost a half century of peace. Gildas is born this same year.
c. 540	Gildas writes *On the Destruction of Britain*.
547–59	Reign of King Ida, First Saxon King of Bernicia.
570	Death of Gildas (according to Irish annals).
573–79	Reign of King Theodric, King of Bernicia.
577	Battle of Dyrham.
586–92	Reign of King Hussa of Bernicia. According to the *Historia Brittonum* he wages war against four British kings: Gwallog, Morgan, Rhydderch Hen, and Urien.
592–616	Reign of King Aethelfrith of Bernicia.
597	Death of St. Columba.

603	Battle of Dagestan: Aethelfrith defeats Áedán mac Gabráin.

c. 604	Aethelfrith assumes control of Deira (creating the joint kingdom of Northumberland). His rival Edwin is driven into exile.
c. 615	Battle of Chester: Aethelfrith defeats Selyf ap Cyan, 'King of the Britons' (actually the ruler of Powys).
616	Death of Aethelberht, the Saxon King of Kent. Battle of River Iddle: Aethelfrith is killed by Raedwald, King of East Anglia, and the exile Edwin, who seizes the crown.
616–33	Reign of King Edwin of Northumbria.
c. 625	Death of Raedwald.
626	Synod of Maçon: supremacy of Catholic Church over its Celtic rival.
627	Baptism of King Edwin of Northumbria.
630	Sigeberht assumes vacant throne of East Anglia.
633	Cadwallon, British King of Gwynedd allies with Penda, a contender to the Northumbrian throne. Battle of Hatfield: King Edwin defeated and killed by Cadwallon. Edwin's son Osric becomes King of Deira, while Eanfrith, son of Aethelfrith seizes control of Bernicia.
634	Cadwallon defeats and kills both King Osric and Eanfrith. Eanfrith's brother Oswald becomes new King of Bernicia. Battle of Denisesburna (or Heavenfield) near Hexham: Cadwallon defeated and killed by Oswald. This marks the end of the last British counter-attack against the English.
635	Foundation of the monastery at Lindisfarne.
c. 638	Siege of Dun Eiden (Edinburgh) – defeat of the Gododdin.

Surmounted by a medieval church, Glastonbury Tor dominates the landscape of the Somerset Levels. A site with strong links to the 'Arthurian' legend, the tor is also the site of a 5th- and 6th-century defended homestead or religious site, although we know little about its form or function. (Steve Beckwith)

THE DESIGN AND FUNCTION OF 'ARTHURIAN' FORTS

There is no clear, simple view of the forts used in Britain during Late Antiquity – no neat linear development to follow, or even demonstrable geographic pattern. Instead we have a mixture of fortification types and styles – some involving the reoccupation of long-abandoned Iron Age hill-forts, and others the patching up and adaptation of abandoned Roman defensive works. We can also add another category to the list: the forts which were built during this period to suit the particular needs of the warlords who fought for control of Britain, and who needed secure bases to operate from. Another form of these were the walls – long linear earthworks designed to mark boundaries.

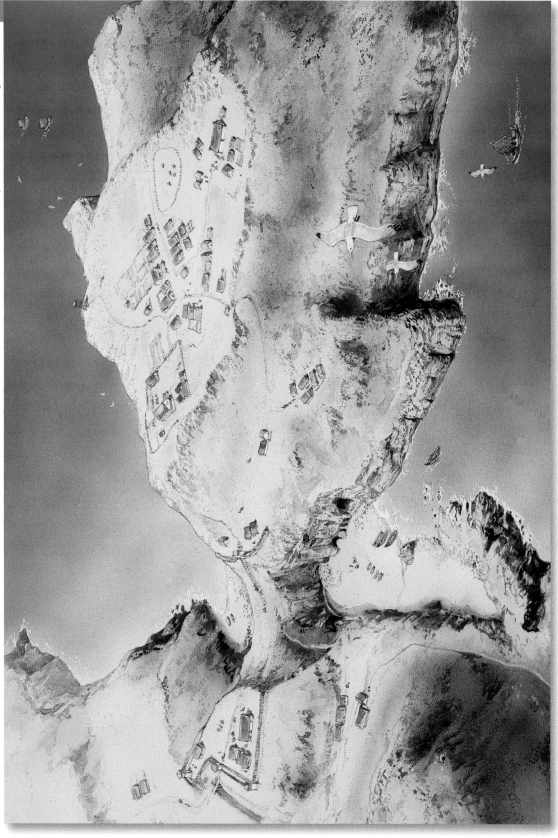

The peninsular fort: Tintagel, Cornwall

A THE PENINSULAR FORT: TINTAGEL, CORNWALL

The spectacular promontory of Tintagel is closely associated with the 'Arthurian' legend, as according to the medieval romantic Geoffrey of Monmouth the fort there was his birthplace, the result of an extra-marital union between Uther Pendragon and Queen Igraine of Cornwall. What we do know is that the peninsula and the landward side of its narrow land bridge were both occupied during Late Antiquity. Excavations conducted during the 1930s revealed the remains of a Celtic monastery on the peninsula, as well as traces of a fortified royal court and domestic or mercantile buildings. The Ravenna Cosmography of c. AD 700 which listed place names around the known world included a mention of Purocoronavis, (a corruption of Durocornovium, 'the Cornish fort'). This may well have been a reference to Tintagel.

The monastery crowned the high point of the peninsula, above the land bridge, while the archaeological remains of a group of buildings closer to the tip of the peninsula were associated with the royal court. Other structures covered much of the rest of the peninsula, while the mainland side of the land bridge was protected by a deep ditch, a stockade perimeter and the spectacular cliffs which made Tintagel a naturally defensible location.

One of the problems here is that there isn't much evidence to go on. As we have seen, the historical records are patchy, confusing and often contradictory. While this is bad enough for the Saxons, the situation is far worse for the Britons, whose lack of detailed written records has led to much of the controversy over the existence of Arthur. Archaeology is a far more reliable source of information, but even here there is little evidence. While a few sites – most notably South Cadbury, Birdoswald, Wroxeter, Bamburgh and Tintagel have all been excavated to some degree, and have produced a wealth of information, this isn't really a sufficient sample. It doesn't allow us to build up a bigger picture, showing what was going on across Britain.

While the archaeological footprint of the Romans in Britain has been the subject of detailed investigation for more than a century, the centuries following the end of Roman rule have been largely ignored. Without solid archaeological evidence historians can – and do – waste large amounts of paper arguing over the existence of Arthur, the reliability of the documentary evidence and even the chronology of events. Fortunately this has improved slightly in recent years, particularly in the field of Anglo-Saxon archaeology, where new evidence has given us a better understanding of these peoples who first came to Britain in the wake of the Romans.

The hill-fort of Liddington Castle in Wiltshire was first built in the Bronze Age, and by the Iron Age it had become a substantial major hill-fort. Despite there being no evidence of activity here during Late Antiquity, Liddington is often proposed as being the site of the Battle of Badonicus (Badon), fought around AD 500. (Marcus Cowper)

This aerial shot of South Cadbury hill-fort clearly shows the impressive scale of the earthwork defences on the fort's south-eastern side. The more substantial bank on the right is the 'Arthurian' rampart, while the two on the front of it date from the Iron Age. During the refortification of the fort in Late Antiquity these outer defences remained in their original condition, although silt may well have been removed from the early ditches. (Camelot Research Committee)

Consequently old notions of 'invasion' and 'conquest' have been replaced with the suggestion that the establishment of Anglo-Saxon supremacy over southern Britain was a gradual process, aided as much by assimilation, trade and marriage as by fire and sword. Certainly there were clashes – including highly notable ones – between the incomers and the locals, but these seem to have been interspersed with long periods of relative calm, and even co-existence. It has recently been suggested that on the east coast of what is now England the Anglo-Saxons simply replaced the existing upper strata of Romano-British society, becoming the new rulers and protectors, while leaving the bulk of the population to continue living much as they had before. However, only further archaeology will prove or disprove this theory, or tell us more about the fortifications used by Britons, Saxons and others within the British Isles.

In the survey of fortifications that follows, I have limited the scope to Britain south of Hadrian's Wall – effectively to the territory that formed the provinces of Roman Britain. Certainly the Romans still maintained a presence farther north, but by the 4th century AD this was largely a matter of maintaining friendly 'buffer states' between Roman Britain and the lands of the Picts and Scots. It is hoped that a companion volume will eventually be produced in this series, which will cover the forts used by these peoples of Northern Britain. Similarly while Ireland has been a source of significant archaeological information about this period, the island really deserves a study all of its own, and so has been omitted from this book.

We know where the Iron-Age hill-forts were, as their remains still exist. For the most part this is also true of the Roman military works which dotted the British landscape – walls, legionary fortresses, coastal forts and fortified towns. Clearly the defensive nature of both these reoccupied hill-forts and the old Roman fortified works were very different, as too were the new breed of defensive positions built during this period. We need to look at each of these three groups in turn before we can get a better picture of their true defensive value, and of how they might have been used by the 'Arthurian' warriors of post-Roman Britain or the followers of the Early Saxon kings.

The hill-fort of Old Sarum, Wiltshire. The *Anglo-Saxon Chronicle* records that in AD 552 the Saxon leader Cynric 'fought against the Britons in a place which is named Searo byrg [Sorbiodunum, or Old Sarum], and put the Britons to flight'. (Marcus Cowper)

Reoccupied hill-forts

The Celtic hill-forts of Iron Age Britain were spectacular defensive sites, and in the inter-tribal warfare which existed in Britain before the coming of the Romans many of them were probably considered invulnerable. However, in AD 43 these impressive looking defensive positions proved no match for the Roman army. That summer General Vespasian led his legion westwards through what is now Hampshire, Wiltshire, Dorset and Somerset, overcoming every fortified site where resistance was offered to the Romans. Hill-forts such as Maiden Castle and Hod Hill were captured with relatively little difficulty, as the Celtic tribesmen who defended them had no answer to the sophisticated torsion-powered siege weapons and techniques that were at Vespasian's disposal.

This same pattern was repeated as the Romans continued their expansion northwards, and in almost every case the victors slighted the defences of the forts they captured – pulling down their palisades, demolishing their gatehouses and destroying whatever buildings of military value were found within the perimeter of these hilltop positions. During the centuries of Roman occupation these forts were abandoned, and instead Roman legionary fortresses provided the bases from which the province was defended. When the Romans left Britain at the start of the 5th century AD these legionary fortresses were largely abandoned, and, as noted earlier, the post-Roman Britons turned to their old strongholds when threatened by Saxon, Pictish, Angle, Jute or Irish invaders.

These old hill-forts that dominated the landscape of Britain before the coming of the Romans were not spread equally throughout Britain, but instead were concentrated into (in pretty rough terms) what is now the south-west of England, in Hampshire and Wiltshire, in Wales, and in the Borders and southern central-belt of Scotland. While there were exceptions – for instance, you can find the remains of small Iron Age forts in Cambridge, Essex and Hertfordshire – the majority conformed to these basic geographical patterns. This means that the people who lived within these regions during Late Antiquity had the option to reoccupy these sites. Large hill-forts existed north of Hadrian's Wall – sites such as Traprain Law, or Dun Eiden (Edinburgh) where archaeological and historical evidence both suggest these served as important regional centres in Late Antiquity. However, while the design and re-use of these forts forms the basis of this study, they lie beyond our geographical boundaries.

Professor Leslie Alcock speculated about the defensive value of these post-Roman hill-forts during his excavation of South Cadbury–Camelot. He surmised that the reoccupied hill-fort at South Cadbury was an extremely important site in 5th and 6th century Dumnonia, which encompassed most of what is now south-western England. In those times the English – the Saxons – lay to the east, and South Cadbury was the cornerstone of British resistance in the region. He argued that the extensive finds of imported pottery support his theory about the importance of the hill-fort within Dumnonia, although he also stressed the dangers of assuming more than the archaeological evidence can tell us. In fact this site was so well-defended in the 5th and 6th century AD that it should really be considered a completely new defensive work.

What is obvious is that a well-defended hill-fort like South Cadbury was an exception; most hill-forts in Britain were considerably smaller, with far less

The Tristan Stone now stands outside Fowey in Cornwall, but was originally erected a few miles away, beside Castle Dore. It is thought it was carved around AD 550, and is inscribed on one side with an early Christian cross, and on the other with a Latinate inscription, which translates as 'Trystan here lies, of Cunomorus the son'. Tristan was the hero of the medieval romance 'Tristan and Isolde'. (Steve Beckwith)

impressive defences. There were also regional variations, as well as differences between coastal and inland sites, or those in mountainous areas and sites in largely rolling countryside. For instance, in Wales it was much more common to use stone as a building tool, largely because it was more readily available on the sites where hill-forts already existed. The use of stone walls in the new generation of hill-forts – places like Dinas Emrys – show how these building traditions simply carried on from the Iron Age into the later period.

There was also a problem with size. The function of the majority of Iron Age hill-forts was to provide a place of refuge for a whole tribal region, or at least for the population of the fort's hinterland. In Late Antiquity it seems that these forts served as bases for local warlords, kings or other military figures, and the local population was left to its own devices. This was less callous than it sounds; as we shall see later, the nature of warfare had changed, and for the most part these warlords and their armies vied for control of the land and its population, leaving everyone else to continue to raise crops and tend their fields, thus providing logistical support for the fighting armies.

Consequently, with a few notable exceptions these hill-forts needed to be smaller than those of the Iron Age, allowing them to be defended by a small professional force. Sites such as Castle Dore in Dumnonia (now Cornwall) were small by comparison with, for example, Maiden Castle in Dorset, but archaeological evidence suggests that this small circular hill-fort was well defended, and contained at least three large, post-Iron Age buildings, presumably designed to house the men and stores needed to maintain the fort as an operational base. Castle Dore – associated with King Mark of the Tristan and Isolde legend – was therefore perfectly suited as the fortified stronghold of a regional king or local warlord.

Finally, we have to consider the apparent differences between fortified sites occupied by the post-Roman Britons and by their enemies. The Anglo-Saxons first landed in Kent and East Anglia, both areas that were not known for their hill-forts. However, the expansion of these Anglo-Saxon enclaves during the 5th and 6th centuries AD into what is now Hampshire and the Thames Valley brought the Saxons into areas noted for such sites as Cissbury, Uffington, Old Sarum, Old Winchester Hill, Beacon Hill and Danebury, which as a result now lay on the frontier between Anglo-Saxon England and post-Roman Britain. It therefore seems highly likely that even if these sites were not extensively re-fortified, they might well have been pressed into service as readily fortifiable camps.

B THE POST-ROMAN BRITISH TOWN: WROXETER (VIROCONIUM), SHROPSHIRE

Located on high ground overlooking the upper reaches of the River Severn, the Roman town of Viroconium (Wroxeter) grew up around a small fort, and in its heyday around the 2nd century AD it was the fourth largest urban centre in Roman Britain. During this period a large bathhouse was built in the town centre, the remains of which can still be seen today. However, the population of the town declined in the centuries that followed, and by the time the Roman army left Britain in the early 5th century AD Wroxeter was more of a regular marketplace than a bustling urban community. The baths and other civic buildings fell into disrepair, and became derelict. Then the fortunes of the town changed.

During the 'Arthurian' period many of the buildings in the town centre were demolished, their foundations levelled, and new buildings erected in their place. The town defences were also repaired, and although this new Late Antiquity settlement was smaller than its Roman predecessor, the town recovered some of its vibrancy. It has been suggested that Wroxeter served as the capital for the post-Roman British rulers of Powys, and that the remains of a substantial 'Arthurian' building which had been built on the site of the Roman baths was the royal court of these important British kings. The city was finally abandoned in the late 7th century AD, and eventually the site returned to pasture. Consequently it represents something of an archaeological marvel – a Roman and post-Roman town which was never disturbed by subsequent phases of occupation.

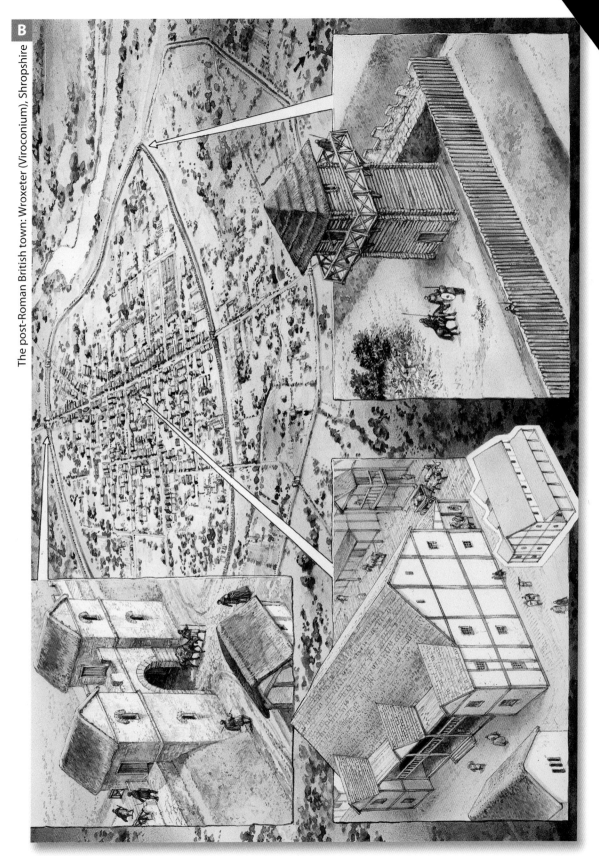

The post-Roman British town: Wroxeter (Viroconium), Shropshire

While there is little archaeological evidence to show that these sites were re-used, their geographical location made them strategically important, and as such it stands to reason that they occasionally served a military purpose, even if it were just to provide a safe temporary refuge for a passing army. Other old forts, such as Bamburgh, were captured by the Saxons, and then refortified as Saxon strongholds. There is evidence of Iron Age activity on the crag that forms the site of Bamburgh Castle, and when the Saxon kings of Bernicia turned the crag into a fortress they must have integrated these earlier defences into their own works. Of course, more archaeological evidence is needed to build up a better picture of the way older forts were re-used during this period, but the potential they offered to Britons and Saxons alike is self-evident.

Reoccupied Roman fortifications

In theory the Roman military presence in Britain was concentrated in the north of the province, with significant garrisons stationed in the legionary fortress at York, and on Hadrian's Wall, protecting Britannia's northern frontier. However, in AD 383 the general Magnus Maximus led the bulk of the Roman field army over to Gaul, and it seems that most of these troops never returned to their old garrisons. During this period the Western Roman Empire was in turmoil; civil war, barbarian invasion and politics all led to a gradual withdrawal of Roman troops from the borders of the empire. Following the death of Emperor Theodosius (AD 395) the situation became steadily worse, and led directly to the sack of Rome 15 years later.

In Britain the old ordered system of office holding and imperial patronage seems to have fallen apart, and a succession of imperial 'usurpers' used the remains of the Roman military presence in Britain for their own ends. This culminated in the campaigns of the usurper Constantine III, who in AD 407 led the remnants of the Roman field army in Britain to Gaul, in a doomed attempt to repulse the 'barbarian invasions' of the previous winter. Although Roman garrison troops remained behind, for the most part these consisted of *limitanei* (border troops), who were second-class soldiers, of limited military value. The nature of these Roman garrisons had also changed over the centuries, and by the start of the 5th century AD they were effectively tied to the defence of static positions. Their families lived with them, either in or beside the fort, and the troops were more likely to live in their own family homes rather than in military barracks.

It has been suggested that in AD 383 Magnus Maximus withdrew the garrisons from Hadrian's Wall, relocating them farther south near York, but whether this involved all or even some of the *limitanei* is open to question. In Wales control of the region was apparently handed over to *foederati* (native allies) – British chieftains – who maintained the peace on behalf of the Romans in the same way that the Britons north of Hadrian's Wall formed a 'buffer state' between the hostile Picts and Scots and the Roman provinces. The likelihood is that Roman garrisons were maintained along Hadrian's Wall until at least AD 407, as coins have been found there dating from the early 5th century AD. However, the Roman economy collapsed soon afterwards, and it was replaced by a barter system. While this worked well in the rural economy of post-Roman Britain, the lack of ready pay would reduce the effectiveness of any remaining garrisons.

It appears that from AD 410 onwards, at least some of the forts of Hadrian's Wall were maintained by local rulers, possibly the existing ruling echelons of Romano-British society. These *civitates* assumed control of any remaining garrisons, and in time it can be assumed that they evolved into the post-Roman warlords and military commanders whose archaeological traces can still be found along Rome's northern frontier. One of these reoccupied forts at Birdoswald in Cumbria has been excavated, revealing that not only was a garrison maintained there, but the local warlord who occupied Birdoswald even built a substantial hall there, a focal point for a post-Roman garrison set amid the crumbling remains of an older Roman stronghold.

It has been suggested that several other forts along Hadrian's Wall were re-used in this way, although convincing archaeological evidence of this has still to be found. This suggests that these forts helped to anchor the local Romano-British community, who faced attacks from the north from the Picts and the Scots, and later from the growing power of the Anglo-Saxon Kingdom of Bernicia, whose base at Bamburgh was close to the eastern end of the wall. Unfortunately there is little evidence that the larger Roman legionary fortresses were re-used, although yet again the archaeological evidence of post-Roman activity was long seen as an irrelevance, as academics concentrated on the more spectacular period which preceded the collapse of Roman power in Britain. The surviving walls of the great fortresses of Eboracum (York), Deva (Chester), Isca Silurum (Caerlon) and Lindensium (Lincoln) suggest that in the 5th and 6th centuries AD these were still impressive places, and it seems inconceivable that local *civitates* or rulers failed to make use of these defences in some way.

In the *Annales Cambrae* (The Welsh Easter Annals) Chester is referred to as *Cair Legion* (the City of the Legions), a name which is also found in the writings of the 9th century British historian Nennius. In it he cites the 'City of the Legions' as the venue for one of Arthur's battles. While the accuracy of Nennius is a matter of vigorous debate, this at least suggests that Chester remained an important location, and its walls provided sanctuary from Irish or Saxon raiders in time of danger.

We are on firmer ground when it comes to another important Roman town. Unlike most other Roman towns, Viroconium (Wroxeter) was abandoned rather than built over, and its remains are unspoiled by later urban

With the exception of the stone wall of the Roman baths basilica, the bulk of the Roman town of Viroconium (Wroxeter) was below the soil before excavation work began. In this photograph the layout of the streets and major buildings can be traced through the sub-soil. (Stratford Archive)

The walls of the Late Roman 'Saxon Shore' fort of Anderitum in Pevensey, Sussex still represent a formidable obstacle some 17 centuries after they were built. However, the *Anglo-Saxon Chronicle* records that the fort was successfully stormed by the Saxon leaders Aelle and Cissa in AD 491, and the defenders were massacred. (Steve Danes)

growth. This 'greenfield' site was meticulously excavated during the 1970s, and this time proper attention was paid to the faint traces of post-Roman activity. In its heyday Wroxeter was a bustling town, whose civic life centred on a substantial baths complex, dominated by a grand basilica. However, by the late 4th century the town was in decline, and the baths had fallen into disuse. The archaeologists discovered that the site was used as a marketplace, where goods were probably bartered rather than bought. It was also a settlement in decline, at least until between AD 530–90, when Wroxeter was transformed. The remains of the basilica were demolished, and the site levelled using thousands of tons of rubble. A large wooden hall was built, its design mimicking Roman civic architecture in wood, while the area around it was built up with more wooden buildings, shops and stores. At the same time the neglected and somewhat rudimentary defences of the town were repaired and strengthened. As these had a circumference of some two miles this was a substantial undertaking, as too was the rebuilding of the city centre. It has been suggested that during the 6th century Wroxeter was the capital of a post-Roman British leader, possibly a king of Powys or even the base of a 'high king'. Given the resources and manpower used to rebuild the town, whoever the ruler was wielded considerable power and influence over post-Roman Britain. If this took place in Wroxeter, then it is possible that other fortified Roman towns or military settlements underwent a similar, albeit probably a less spectacular, transformation.

That leaves us with the enigma of the Roman forts of the Saxon Shore. This chain of 11 fortresses was built along the eastern and southern coast of what is now England, from the Wash in Norfolk round to the Solent in Hampshire. These were impressive structures, and represent a significant outlay of resources. They were built in the mid 3rd century AD, and remained in use until the first decade of the 5th century AD, if not later. They were listed in the *Notitia Dignitatum* (*List of High Offices*), a late 4th-century catalogue of Roman military resources, which states that they fell under the command of the *Comes Litoris Saxonici* (Count of the Saxon Shore). This is what gave the strongholds their name, rather than any role they might have played in repelling a Saxon landing.

In recent years the assumption that these forts were built as a response to Saxon raiders has been questioned. They contain little evidence of Roman military activity, and it seemed that they had no permanent garrison. It has been argued that they were little more than fortified storehouses, although quite why the Romans would go to the trouble of making these so imposing still has to be explained. However, at least we have evidence of their use after the departure of the Roman army from Britain. The *Anglo-Saxon Chronicle* records that in AD 491 'Aelle and Cissa besieged Andredes Cester, and killed all who lived in there; there was not even one Briton left.' Andredes Cester was a Saxon name for Anderitum (Pevensey) in East Sussex, the largest of all the Saxon Shore forts. Clearly a post-Roman British garrison was maintained within the walls of the crumbling fortress, and it proved unable to prevent the Saxons from breaching the defences. One suspects that the garrison was simply too small to effectively defend such a substantial fortification.

OPPOSITE PAGE
This map shows the location of the known key fortified sites in 'Arthurian' Britain. Other major sites mentioned in the text are also indicated.

Key fortified sites in 'Arthurian' Britain

Lindisfarne
Bamburgh

High Rochester

Birdoswald   Hadrian's Wall

BERNICIA

RHEGED

NORTHUMBRIA

Catterick

DEIRA

Ouse

York

LINDSEY

Trent

Lincoln

Castell
Degannwy

Chester

Dinas Emrys   Dee

Garn Baduan

GWYNEDD   POWYS

Wroxeter

MERCIA

EAST
ANGLIA

Nene

Gt Ouse

DYFED   GWENT

WESSEX

Colchester

Severn

Gloucester

Cirencester

St Albans

ESSEX

Caerlon

Dinas Powys

Cadbury-
Congresbury

Bath

Thames

London

KENT

Old Sarum

South
Cadbury

Winchester

SUSSEX

Tintagel   DUMNONIA

KERNOW   Castle Dore

Chun

N

| 0 | 50 miles |
| 0 | 100km |

Others have suggested that some other Saxon Shore forts were pressed into service during this period. For instance, it has been argued that Walton Castle (now submerged off the Suffolk coast) served as a local post-Roman British base during the attempt to contain the Saxons in East Anglia, while others such as Portus Adurni (Portchester) were garrisoned as a means of protecting a particular stretch of the southern coast. We know all too little about the role these forts played in Late Antiquity, and so however logical they may be, many of these theories remain little more than conjecture. For a more detailed discussion of these fortifications, see *Rome's Saxon Shore* (Osprey Fortress 56).

ABOVE
The legend of Dinas Emrys. Reputedly this fortress in Gwynedd was built on the site of a pit, which contained two dragons, engaged in a fight to the death. As Vortigern watched the red dragon (representing the British) emerged victorious over its white enemy (which represented the Saxons). (Stratford Archive)

BELOW
The main hill-fort of Garn Boduan in the Lleyn Peninsula dates from the Iron Age, but in the 5th century AD a far smaller stone-walled fort was built on the highest part of the site, on the eastern side of the hill. (After RCAMW)

The sites of Late Antiquity

A final category covers fortifications that were built during this period rather than simply reoccupied. While this appears to have been rare, the post-Roman Britons of Powys, Brycheiniog and Gwynedd often elected to construct new forts, designed to protect their Welsh mountain strongholds from Saxon attack. This was probably because many of the existing Iron Age sites were in the wrong place, clustered for the most part near the coast of the Irish Sea, rather than blocking valleys and approach routes that entered Wales from the east.

A prime example of this kind of fort is Dinas Emrys (called 'the Fortress of Ambrosius' by Gildas) in the Snowdonia region of Gwynedd. Built on the summit of a small crag, this fort takes advantage of a superb natural defensive position, as there are only two approaches to the summit. The stone-built ramparts follow the line of the summit rather than any defensive scheme, and the circuit is interrupted by rocky outcrops, giving the whole fort a slightly ramshackle appearance. However, this belies the defensive qualities of the site; in the 5th and 6th centuries AD Dinas Emrys would have been nigh-on impregnable. The fort itself is traditionally linked with Ambrosius Aurelianus, the Romano-British leader praised by Gildas for offering organized resistance to the Saxons. In Welsh legend he is known as Emrys Wledig, although other sources suggest that Ambrosius was based in what is now southern England rather than the Welsh mountains.

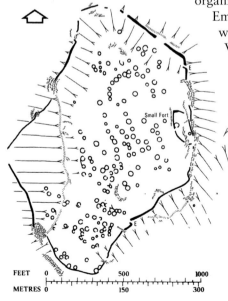

Dinas Emrys is also linked to the post-Roman British ruler (or 'tyrant') Vortigern, the man whom the *Anglo-Saxon Chronicle* claims invited the Saxons to Britain in the first place. In his 11th-century *Historia Regum Britanniae* Geoffrey of Monmouth claimed that Vortigern ordered a fortress to be built on the crag, but the walls kept on collapsing. Druids advised him to sacrifice a 'fatherless boy', and to sprinkle the walls with his blood. When a suitable victim was chosen the child turned out to be a prophet and magician – none other than Merlin. He claimed that the reason the walls refused to stand was that they were built over a hidden pool. Vortigern ordered his men to dig, and they revealed an underground chamber, where a red and a white dragon were locked in combat. As they watched, the red dragon (representing the Britons) vanquished its rival (who was

The Devil's Dyke (or St. Edmund's Dyke) ran for almost eight miles (13km), spanning the Icknield Way in East Anglia near the modern town of Newmarket, Suffolk. In Late Antiquity this Anglo-Saxon barrier bridged the land between the marshes bordering the River Cam to the west and the forest to the east. (Sam Marks)

taken to represent the Saxons). Today the same red dragon of legend is prominently displayed on the Welsh flag.

While a charming tale, like most of Geoffrey of Monmouth's writing it has only a passing link to fact. It was gleaned from Nennius's *Historia Brittonum* (chapters 40–42), but even then it appears to be a retelling of an earlier apocryphal tale. However, when the hilltop was excavated in the 1950s an underground cistern or pool was discovered, in the centre of the plateau. It was constructed in Late Antiquity, as were the thick dry-stone walls that ringed the crag. One suspects that this was a case of legend imitating fact: the pool was a known feature, and so it became the basis for the Welsh legend. The story was created to fit the visible remains of the site. While the legend itself is interesting, it does little to further our understanding of the site, save to reinforce the notion that Dinas Emrys was regarded as an important stronghold during the centuries following the Roman departure from Britain.

The walls encircling the plateau are some 10ft (3m) thick in places – a formidable defensive barrier. Another outer wall lower down the slope covers the main approach to the summit, while a small second approach – a narrow path climbing a narrow spine-like ridge – was forced to pass beneath the walls for some distance, making a frontal assault virtually impossible. All this building effort suggests that whoever built Dinas Emrys was able to draw upon a considerable pool of manpower and resources.

There is at least one notable geographical exception to the notion that most of the newly built forts of Late Antiquity were built to cover eastern approaches through the Welsh mountains. The small hill-fort on the summit of Garn Boduan, on the Lleyn Peninsula in Gwynedd, overlooks the sea, and would have provided a secure refuge in the event of an attack by Irish raiders or pirates. The dry-stone wall encircling the perimeter is substantial, enclosing an area of some 10 hectares (25 acres), although this

The small fort of Dinas Emrys was built on top of a 250ft-high (75m) crag overlooking the River Glaslyn in Gwynedd. The site took full advantage of its superb natural position to render its defences virtually impregnable. (After RCAMW)

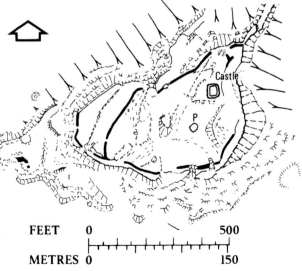

FEET   0   500

METRES 0   150

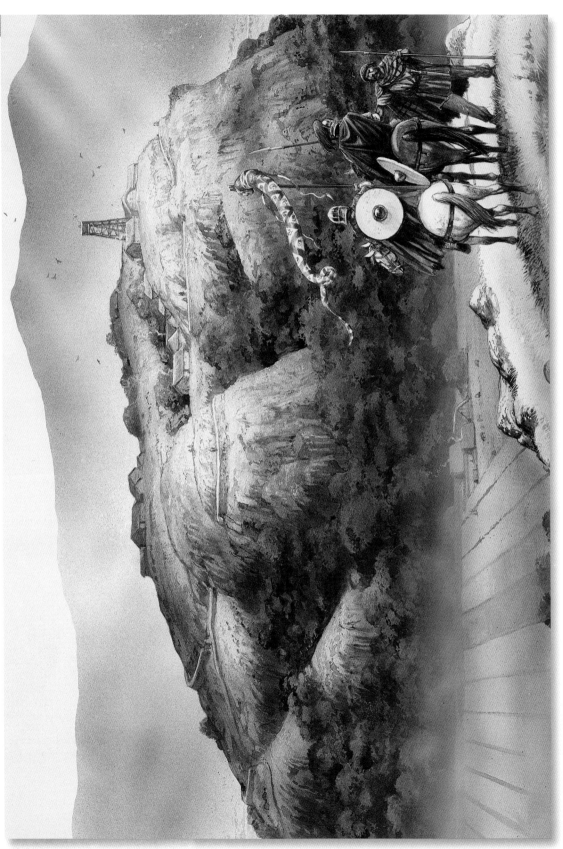

The mountain retreat: Dinas Emrys, Gwynedd, Wales

Another spectacular location for an 'Arthurian' fortress, Dinas Emrys was built on top of an isolated crag overlooking a river, in the mountains of Snowdonia. Legend has associated the site with both Vortigern and Ambrosius Aurelianus, the two historical figures who were supposedly responsible for inviting the Saxons to Britain, and in limiting their expansion westwards. It was also the location for several myths, including one concerning an underground chamber or pool where two dragons fought each other, the existence of which was meant to have been revealed by the young Merlin.

The thick stone walls of the hilltop fortress were built around the rim of the crag, broken in places to take advantage of natural rock outcrops to augment the man-made defences. The circuit was broken by two openings – not even fortified gateways – in the north-east and west sides of the crag. The approaches to these entrances were protected by the shape of the hill – to the west an outer wall covered the main approach to the hill, while on the far side access was provided by a pathway, climbing up the back of a narrow rocky spine. Both approaches would have been covered by the missile fire of the defenders.

is almost certainly an Iron Age structure. The remains of over 170 Celtic roundhouses can be traced on the summit. However, the summit of the hill lies on its eastern side, and it is here that another smaller fort was built, whose walls were far more substantial than those elsewhere on Garn Boduan.

This later fort is post-Roman, and has provisionally been dated to the 7th century AD. It has two entrances, one on its western side and the other on its shorter southern side. The fort is elliptical in plan, and traces of a small round guardhouse can be found set beside the western entrance. There are signs that this entranceway was blocked up while the fort was still in use, and that the southern entrance was enlarged. Apart from that we know little about the site, although the name Garn Boduan has tentatively been linked to Buan, a mythological inhabitant of Gwynedd during this period. Technically Garn Boduan is not a pure Late Antiquity site, as it was set in the corner of an earlier Iron Age hill-fort. However the same could be said of other sites, such as Woden Law in the Scottish Borders, or Cissbury in Sussex. In all these cases the later fort was much smaller than the Iron Age one in which it was located, and should really be seen as a defensive work in its own right.

A reconstruction of the Devil's Dyke, as it would have looked in the 6th century AD. Archaeologists have surmised that the bank was surmounted by a simple wicker boundary fence, and preceded by a substantial ditch. This view gives an impression of how the crossing point over the Icknield Way would have looked, viewed from the west. (Sam Marks)

Unlike the Devil's Dyke a few miles to the north, the bank of Fleam Dyke near Cambridge is less than two metres high, barely enough to present any form of obstacle. This 6th-century Anglo-Saxon earthwork should be seen as a boundary rather than as a military obstacle. (Sam Marks)

A similar argument could be given for larger sites of Late Antiquity, such as South Cadbury–Camelot, Tintagel, Bamburgh, Chun Castle, Castle Dore, Tre'r Ceiri, Dinas Powys or Cadbury–Congresbury. In all these cases an existing Iron Age fort was adapted for use during the 5th and 6th centuries AD, and it could be argued that in cases where the defensive qualities of the site were greatly enhanced, it should be seen as a fort of Late Antiquity in its own right. For example, there is little evidence for the Iron Age occupation of the fortified crag at Bamburgh, but during the 7th century AD it was transformed into the royal seat of the Anglo-Saxon kings of Bernicia. Almost all traces of an earlier settlement were swept away in the construction of a new stronghold, and so Bamburgh should be categorized as a fortress of Late Antiquity rather than a refortified enclosure from an earlier age.

Of course there were other sites that were built close to earlier works, probably in an attempt to reinforce the point that a new power was in charge of the region. A prime example is the 7th-century Saxon palace at Yeavering (also known as Ad Gefrin), a site which in turn was dominated by an abandoned British hill-fort on the summit of Yeavering Bell. It was once thought that a semi-fortified enclosure next to the palace was an earlier Saxon fort, but it now seems more likely that it was simply a livestock enclosure, or even the site of a gathering associated with the collection of taxes or dues. What this demonstrates is that by the end of the 'Arthurian' period this area was considered safely within the borders of Saxon territory. Yeavering is defended not by ditches and palisades, but by territory – the Kingdom of Northumberland. The site has been associated with King Edwin (AD 616–33), who converted to Christianity in AD 627, shortly before his death at the Battle of Hatfield.

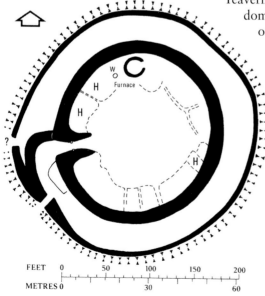

Less of a hill-fort than a fortified homestead, Chun Castle on the western tip of Cornwall was another Iron Age site which was refortified in Late Antiquity. The circular defences encompassed a courtyard, ringed by smaller buildings. (After RCAM)

FEET 0   50   100   150   200

METRES 0   30   60

Finally there are the dykes – long linear barriers that crossed large stretches of the countryside. The most substantial was the Wodnesdic (Wansdyke), which stretches through Wiltshire and Somerset. The name – associated with Woden – suggests that it existed before the conversion of the Saxons of Wessex around AD 630. In fact it is divided into two sections – the East and West Wansdyke – with a 15-mile gap in between. Professor Alcock suggested that the eastern section may have been built as a defensive barrier by the Britons of Dumnonia, protecting them from the Saxons of the Thames Valley. He saw the western stretch as a later addition, constructed by either the Britons or the Saxons in the aftermath of the Battle of Dyrham (AD 577), and therefore dates to the same period as South Cadbury–Camelot.

In Cambridgeshire a series of dykes ran across the old pre-Roman road known as the Icknield Way, and were probably designed to bridge the gap between the boggy fens to the west and the forests to the west. They have been associated with the Saxons of East Anglia – a series of defensive lines to deter British raiders, or to mark different phases of a frontier. The modern euphemism for these structures is 'separation barrier', and this is how they should probably be viewed. They were no more defensible than, say, the modern Mexico–USA border, but they were designed to mark a boundary. Their length could be patrolled to deter interlopers, while crossing points would be guarded. While they would have offered some defensive value to a defender, they were hardly insurmountable obstacles, particularly as none of these structures have ever been associated with a permanent garrison, like the ones found on Hadrian's Wall. Instead these were a means of marking territory – a political statement rather than a military one.

A TOUR OF SOUTH CADBURY–CAMELOT

A fairly wide range of fort types existed in Early Medieval Britain, from crumbling Roman towns, re-fortified Celtic hill-forts, to promontory forts and earthwork *limes*. Of these the most important were the hill-forts, symbols of regional power before the coming of the Romans, and reoccupied after the Romano-British were left to their own devices. One of the largest and most important of these sites is South Cadbury in Somerset, a hill-fort which was extensively excavated during the 1970s, and which yielded some surprising information on the nature of fortifications in 'Arthurian' Britain.

The site itself had probably been occupied since the early Neolithic period, around 3000 BC, and by the 5th century BC Cadbury Hill had become the site of a substantial settlement, protected by a wooden palisade and an outer ditch which ran around the edge of the plateau. There were also signs that the hill had some form of religious significance: archaeologists found signs of religious activity, including the deliberate and ritual destruction of a bronze

The hill-fort of South Cadbury, as it looked in 1723, in an engraving by the antiquarian William Stukeley. This view from the north-west exaggerates the size and number of the fort's outer ramparts. (Stratford Archive)

The hill-fort of South Cadbury, viewed from the south during the 1970 excavation, which concentrated on the site of the 'Arthurian' great hall in the centre of the defensive perimeter. (Camelot Research Committee)

shield. By the time the Romans arrived in Britain in the mid 1st century AD Cadbury was defended by an impressive complex of four banks and four ditches. The hill-fort was probably captured by General Vespasian in AD 43, and there is archaeological evidence that the population was put to the sword and the defences torn down. It has also been suggested that it remained the *oppidum* or hill-fort capital of the local ruler Arviragus, who was finally evicted following a minor rebellion against Roman rule during the late 1st century AD.

The hill-fort lay abandoned for more than two centuries, a period when the nearby Roman town of Lindinis (Ilchester) assumed the role of local administrative centre and regional marketplace. However, a small Roman shrine or temple was built on the hilltop, possibly designed to take advantage of the earlier religious associations with the site. Then in the late 3rd century or early 4th century AD there were signs of renewed activity at Cadbury. This was the time when the Roman military garrison in Britain was recalled to the European mainland, and the inhabitants of Roman Britain were left to their own devices. The old hill-fort was pressed into service once again. After all, it had once stood as a symbol of power in the region, and its occupation would have provided legitimacy to its occupier.

The ditches were re-dug, the ramparts were enlarged, and new wooden palisades were built to protect the circuit of the Cadbury defences. Archaeologists had previously suggested that the reoccupation of the hill-fort took place later, around AD 470, and that the defences were expanded around AD 550. This tied in with the 'Arthurian' period, and in 1542 the Tudor antiquary John Leland (1506–52) wrote that:

At the very south end of the church of South-Cadbyri standeth Camallate, sometime a famous town or castle … The people can tell nothing there but that they have heard Arthur much resorted to Camalat.

The 'Arthurian' ramparts of South Cadbury hill-fort were founded on a bed of timber-laced stone rubble, faced with a dry-stone wall. This view taken during the 1970 excavation shows the front face of the rampart base, and the marker poles indicate the location of upright timber supports. (Camelot Research Committee)

This association with Arthurian Camelot remained popular, and during the late 1960s the archeological discovery that Cadbury Hill had been an important fortified site during the 'Arthurian' period only helped to strengthen the link. All that can be said with any certainty is that around AD 600 the hill-fort at Cadbury was a well-fortified and vibrant site, possibly the seat of a ruler of considerable regional importance. Consequently it has been suggested that, although an 'Arthurian' connection cannot be proved, Cadbury–Camelot was the principal stronghold of the King of Dumnonia, the Romano-British ruler who controlled what is now the English West Country.

A visitor to Cadbury approached the fort on a cobbled road which passed through at an entrance located in its south-western corner. Another secondary entrance was located on the north-eastern side of the hill-fort. The western entrance was clearly the main one, but, unlike the complex, chicaned approach found at the nearby Maiden Castle hill-fort, Cadbury could be approached without having to thread through the sequence of outer banks and ditches. Instead the visitor would be faced with an impressive gateway. All the earthen ramparts pre-dated the Romano-British reoccupation of the fort, and all of them had formed part of the fort's defensive system when Cadbury was captured by the Roman army in AD 43. There is no archaeological evidence to suggest that during the 'Arthurian' period these outer banks were augmented by palisades, but it is possible that a light wooden palisade might have served to channel or slow any attackers, or served as protection for defending archers or javelin men.

The innermost bank was revetted on its inner side by a dry-stone wall, which probably dated from this earlier phase of occupation. However, instead of being surmounted by a simple wooden palisade this bank was crowned by a substantial wooden wall, set in a layer of dressed masonry, and backed by an earthen and rubble platform or walkway. The archaeological excavation of this feature which took place between 1966 and 1970 has resulted in the reconstruction of these 'Arthurian' defences. The wall itself was anchored by a series of stout posts, set into stone-lined postholes around 3ft (0.9m) deep. These were then linked by the dressed stone blocks mentioned above, with the lower courses consisting of the largest rectangular blocks of cut and shaped stone.

A second line of postholes about 6ft (1.8m) behind the first probably mark the location of the shorter posts which formed the rear edge of the rampart walkway. These also served to support wooden cross-braces which linked these posts to the main uprights directly in front of them. The result was a simple wooden lattice with a front face of dressed stone. The space inside this lattice was filled with stones and rubble, raising the level of the original Iron Age bank by some 5ft (1.5m). This raised bank was also extended backwards behind the rear posts before the bank dropped off towards the inner side of the fort. The entire raised bank was some 16ft (4.8m) thick at its base – where it met the top of the older bank. It has been suggested that posts in the front line were about 14 or 15ft (4.2–4.5m) long, which meant they extended as much as 6ft (1.8m) above the

An archaeologist is seen excavating the remains of the 'Arthurian' gatehouse in the south-west corner of the South Cadbury hill-fort. The area in which he is kneeling is the site of the roadway, where it passed through the wooden gatehouse structure. The vertical section behind him marks the line of the fort's inner palisade. (Camelot Research Committee)

top of the stone-fronted raised bank. These were clad in timbers, laid horizontally, and fastened to the upright posts to form a wooden wall.

Elements of this form of construction are similar to those used by Roman engineers to construct the German defences of the Roman Empire, and other simple fortified structures. A plausible reconstruction of the Cadbury defences shows these finished in the Late Roman style, with regular crenellations in the wooden wall, and the rubble-filled space behind them augmented by the addition of a wooden walkway. The whole structure would have been a far more impressive obstacle than the Iron Age defences which had lined the same bank two centuries before, and the elevated fighting platform it provided would have given the defenders a significant advantage over any attacker. These defensive qualities were of course enhanced by the ditch which lay immediately in front of the wall, and by the sequence of three more ditches and banks which lay in front of this inner ditch. Then of course there was the hill itself, whose steep sides would have made a direct assault by a 'Dark Age' aggressor a virtually suicidal proposition.

The western gatehouse was even more impressive than the wall. Archaeology has revealed that it was built around four substantial upright posts, set in a rectangular pattern with its shorter sides facing the inner wall of the fort and its longer sides forming the gateway itself. This box constituted the gatehouse, and, although its original height could not be determined, its scale suggests it was an impressive structure. The front of the gatehouse was fitted with a pair of hinged wooden doors, opening inwards, with a combined span of approximately 10ft (3m). Another matching set of doors on the far side of the gatehouse opened outwards onto the interior of the fort.

The gatehouse itself was set in the original gap in the inner bank of the hill-fort, presumably on the site of an older and far less substantial Iron Age gatehouse. The wall which surmounted this inner ditch joined the gatehouse, and the archaeologists have suggested that it maintained the original lines of the defensive wall, despite the gap in the inner bank. This was most probably achieved by extending the raised bank from the ditch to the two shorter ends of the gatehouse structure, complete with its timber lattice framework, outer facing of dressed stone and infill of rubble. It is assumed that the top of this raised bank reached the same height as the top of the gatehouse, and the wooden palisade was extended to the same height as on the fort's inner banks.

This tentative reconstruction of the 'Arthurian' gatehouse in the south-western corner of South Cadbury hill-fort is based more on the dimensions of the structure than any firm knowledge of its detailed appearance. The artist has clearly based it on Late Roman examples found in the German *limes*. (Camelot Research Committee)

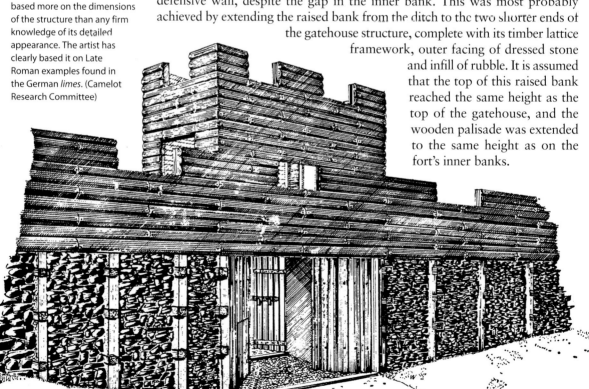

However, the archaeologists also suggest that the gatehouse itself was substantial enough to support a small wooden tower, sited directly over the gatehouse itself – in effect forming an additional storey to the structure. Leslie Alcock, who directed the excavation, has pointed to similar gatehouse structures on Hadrian's Wall and in Roman fortifications in Scotland, where a single tower was raised over the gatehouse. He argued that the structure would probably have had a distinctly Roman appearance, which in turn would have reinforced the link between the fort's occupants and the authority and civic order of the Romans who ruled southern Britain half a century before.

However, other aspects of the defences betray a lack of Roman engineering skill. Although the stone used to form the base of the fort's walls consisted of a face of dressed stone, most of which had once formed part of Roman buildings and which had been gathered for the

The excavation of the banked defences of South Cadbury hill-fort, photographed during the excavation season of 1967. The 'Arthurian' bank is on the skyline. (Camelot Research Committee)

purposes of building the fort's defences, these stones were placed together to form a dry-stone wall, rather than bonded together using mortar, in the Roman fashion. Similarly, the fort itself was irregular in shape, and its 1,200-yard (1,100m) perimeter formed a shape approximating to an oval, following the line of the crest of the plateau. In this respect it was distinctly un-Roman. It has already been suggested that Cadbury Hill had long held significance with the local Celtic Britons as a place of political and possibly religious significance. It therefore made perfect sense for its new occupants to reoccupy the hill-fort and to rebuild the original fortifications where they stood, but also to attempt to reinterpret these defences in a Roman style.

Once the visitor passed through the gate he emerged onto a broad, open plateau which sloped gently towards the centre or summit of the hill. The entire area enclosed by the inner wall was approximately 18 acres (7.3 hectares) – a fairly substantial area of land. The summit itself was crowned by a great timber hall with a thatched roof – labelled 'Arthur's Palace' by the

D **NEXT PAGE: THE SITE OF CAMELOT? THE 'ARTHURIAN' HILL-FORT OF SOUTH CADBURY, WILTSHIRE**

The hill-fort of South Cadbury still dominates the rich farmland around it, much as it would have done during Late Antiquity. The almost circular hill rises steeply towards a plateau, around which the inner defensive wall of the hill-fort was built. This encompassed an area of some 18 acres (7.3 hectares), making it comparable in size to some of the largest hill-forts of Iron Age Britain. However, while South Cadbury was occupied during the Iron Age, it was reoccupied during the 5th century AD, and it was extensively refortified around AD 500 – the time of the Battle of Badon. Archaeologists have a fairly good idea of what the outer walls, which are shown in the upper left inset here, looked like. The base of the rampart consisted of stone rubble, interlaced with wooden beams, while the outer side of the bank was faced with dry-stone walling. The

impression gained by the archaeologists who excavated it is that this walling was constructed fairly hastily, suggesting that the work was undertaken in response to a perceived Saxon threat.

The interior of the fort was dominated by an 'Arthurian' great hall (shown in detail in the lower right inset), the remains of which were discovered on the highest point of the summit, while several buildings, which may have been ancillary buildings, were discovered behind it. Although later Saxon buildings on the plateau coupled with later ploughing have removed traces of many of the 'Arthurian' era buildings within the fort perimeter, the evidence points to South Cadbury being a busy place during the period, combining the functions of a secular administrative centre with those of a military base.

This reconstruction of an Anglo-Saxon village in West Stow in Suffolk is based on sound archaeological evidence. It also provides us with an idea of what the buildings inside the perimeter of a British or Saxon fortification might have looked like during this period. (Stratford Archive)

This reconstruction of the 'Arthurian' defences of the South Cadbury hill-fort shows how the upper wooden palisade was constructed on top of a bank of stone rubble, interlaced with timber supports, and faced by dry-stone walling. (Camelot Research Committee)

press at the time of its excavation, but certainly serving as the residence of an important 5th- or 6th-century ruler. The hall itself was rectangular, 63ft (19.2m) long and 34ft (10.4m) wide, its dimensions revealed by postholes cut into the limestone bedrock. A trench running across the building formed the foundation for a partition wall, dividing the hall into two chambers, one much smaller than the other, and conforming to the idea of a reception hall and adjacent private chambers. This second chamber was separated from the main hall by a passageway running along one wall, and might even have been a kitchen area. Unfortunately the site has been ploughed over during the intervening centuries, so traces of any hearth area could not be located. However, it is all too easy to imagine the great hall itself filled with 'Arthurian' warriors, celebrating, feasting and planning their next campaign against the Saxons.

Like any other buildings located within the Cadbury–Camelot perimeter, the hall would have been covered with a roof structure consisting of wooden beams supported by a row of central wooden posts, and then covered with thatch. Some 12ft (3.6m) north of the great hall the archaeologists found traces of a smaller rectangular building, 12ft (3.6m) long and 6ft (1.8m) wide. The quantities of pottery fragments found in this area suggest that this small ancillary building was probably some form of kitchen store. Unfortunately this is the only other building whose location has been fully examined at Cadbury–Camelot. Given the size and importance of the site it can be

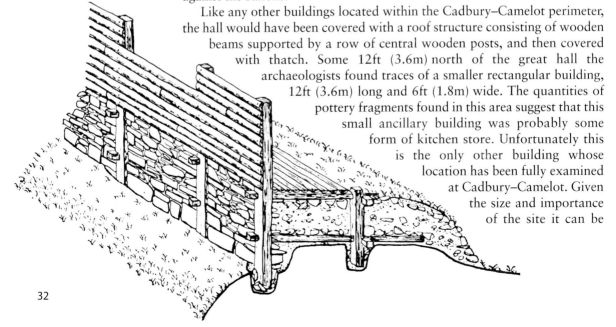

assumed that the plateau would have contained dozens or even hundreds of other buildings of various types – dwellings, storerooms, workshops, armouries, stables, granaries and even a church. However, at present the identity, function and location of any of these buildings is a matter of pure speculation.

In the wake of John Leyland's linking the site with Camelot, the site has developed its fair share of Arthurian associations. It is claimed that Arthur lies buried in a cave beneath the hill, either waiting for a time of great peril, or else emerging for an annual ghostly tour of his old capital. Others point to the proximity of Glastonbury, with its mysterious tor, and the nearby abbey where the medieval monks claimed that Arthur and Guinevere had been buried. Then there is the nearby River Cam, said by some to be the site of Arthur's final battle at Camlann. In truth these stories would probably have passed Cadbury by it were not for Leyland, and the birth of the earlier medieval legends.

None of this bears much scrutiny, leaving us with the hard archaeological evidence, which shows that Cadbury–Camelot was an important location in 'Arthurian' Britain. The site probably served as a permanent administrative centre and fortress, as well as a site capable of sustaining a small 5th- or 6th-century AD army throughout the long winter. While numerous other hill-forts were reoccupied during this period, none shows evidence of having been refortified on such a grand scale. The five seasons of archaeological excavation conducted by Professor Alcock and his team from 1966 to 1970 revealed a small part of the site, and much more remains to be discovered. While academics are all too willing to dismiss any association of Cadbury Hill with the Arthur of legend, Alcock and his team have revealed that whoever it was who refortified the hill-fort was a ruler of great significance to the Britons during the century following the departure of the Romans.

This reconstruction of the 'Arthurian' great hall, whose archaeological remains were found on the summit of the South Cadbury plateau, is based on the relatively solid evidence of posthole size and distribution. Other elements of construction have been gleaned from evidence found elsewhere in Britain and Europe. (Camelot Research Committee)

THE LIVING SITES

The forts which dotted the landscape of Britain in Late Antiquity existed for a reason. Some provided refuge to the local population when danger threatened, while others acted as strongpoints, designed to deter an invader. Others – the more prestigious sites – were centres of power, the seats of kings and rulers. Some were served by a permanent garrison, while others were used only when they were needed. Some sites have yielded sufficient archaeological evidence to allow us to understand what went on in daily life, while in other forts we have no idea how they were used, or even who used them.

We know enough to build up a picture of life in post-Roman Britain, and in the Anglo-Saxon kingdoms that lay along Britain's eastern seaboard. In a number of cases archaeology has allowed us to glimpse something of life within some of these fortifications, and has revealed a little about the role these sites had within Britain during these troubled times. In some cases we can augment the archaeological evidence with information provided by contemporary references, such as the written sources mentioned in the introduction, poetry and even some clerical documentation. In this period we need all the reliable help we can get.

Welsh legal documents from the 6th century AD list the buildings which ought to form part of a royal court – a great hall and private chambers, a

When the Emperor Hadrian ordered the construction of a defensive wall across Britain in the 2nd century AD, Banna (or Birdoswald) was chosen as the location for one of the 16 forts designed to strengthen the linear defences, and to house the wall's garrison. When completed the fort contained barracks, administration buildings, granaries and a headquarters within its rectangular perimeter. Over the centuries a *vicus* or civilian settlement grew up outside its walls.

Following the departure of the Roman army from Britain in the early 5th century AD the fort may have been abandoned, as many of its main buildings quickly fell into disrepair. However,

there are some indications of some form of continued occupation, either by the civilians from the *vicus* or else by a local post-Roman garrison. Around AD 500 a substantial, wood-built great hall was constructed on top of the foundations of one of the fort's two granary buildings. It has been suggested that by the 6th century AD Birdoswald had become the base of a local post-Roman British warlord, and this hall represented his court. If so then Birdoswald had become an important stronghold, and the men who operated from it were well placed to contain the westward expansion of the Saxons of Bernicia.

kitchen, a chapel, a barn, a kiln-house for grain, a stable, a porch and a privy. A site like South Cadbury or Bamburgh would have contained all of these buildings, clustered around the great hall in the centre of the site. That would form the nucleus of the buildings within the fortification, while other buildings – houses or barracks, stables, granaries and workshops – would have filled much of the rest of any defended perimeter. We don't know for certain that South Cadbury was the capital of a Dumnonian king or warlord, but given the impressive scale of the fort and its great hall, then that would be a likely assumption. Buildings of this kind served a very clear purpose, as the focal points of a warrior society.

For both Briton and Saxon this was a period where there was a clearly defined social pyramid, at the apex of which was a warrior king. The inhabitants of Celtic Britain were ruled by kings – and the odd queen – before the coming of the Romans, and it appears that the system was adopted after the Romans left Britain in the early 5th century AD. We also know very little about the transition from a Roman civil administration to a kingdom ruled by a king, although writers like Gildas and Nennius have suggested that rulers like Vortigern combined the prestige of Roman authority with that of a monarchy. Gildas describes Vortigern as a *superbus tyrannus*, which could

These stones mark the foundations of the circular 5th- or 6th-century AD building which stood in the centre of the hill-fort of Cadbury–Congresbury, Somerset. The fort was reoccupied and refortified during this period, and this building was probably the central structure of the 'Arthurian' fortress. (Steve Beckwith)

E

translate as a 'grand tyrant', but more likely means a 'usurper', making him more akin to Magnus Maximus than to a hereditary monarch. This implies that his rule involved the assumption of control of what remained of Roman civil administration. It is likely that subsequent post-Roman British rulers also looked towards the Romans to help justify their position.

The second implication of the Gildas phrase is that Vortigern was a 'high king', and therefore was owed fealty by lesser sub-kings. This model of kingship was certainly practised in Ireland during this period, while in the Saxon kingdoms the *Anglo-Saxon Chronicle* mentions a few rulers who assumed the Saxon title of Bretwalda ('Ruler of Britain') at various times, including Aelle of Sussex, Aethelberht of Kent, Raedwald of East Anglia and Edwin of Northumberland. In the lands of post-Roman Britain the old Celtic tribal divisions re-emerged as small kingdoms, the most notable of which were Dumnonia in what is now south-west England, Powys on the northern Welsh borders, and Gwynedd in the north-west of Wales. We know little about these rulers, or their relative importance to each other, but what isn't revealed in the sparse written records can be gleaned from archaeology.

For instance, substantial amounts of imported pottery have been found during the excavations of the 5th-century stronghold of Dinas Powys, near the modern city of Cardiff, at South Cadbury, at nearby Glastonbury Tor and Cadbury–Congresbury hill-fort, and in the nearby Roman town of Ilchester. Farther to the west the promontory fort and monastic settlement of Tintagel seems to have been a major importer of pottery from Continental Europe, while other pieces have also been found at Castle Dore, and at the small hill-fort at Chun at the western tip of Cornwall. In Wales imported 5th- and 6th-century pottery was also discovered at Dinas Emrys and Castell Degannwy in Gwynedd. All this suggests that these sites were considered important enough during Late Antiquity to contain wealthy post-Roman patrons, with the money and influence to import goods from overseas.

There are other signs of economic activity. Dinas Powys was known to be an important royal stronghold in south-eastern Wales, and its rulers probably dominated much of the Welsh hinterland and even the Severn Valley. Its excavation yielded substantial amounts of imported pottery, but also evidence of activity directly linked to a royal court, such as jewel-making, metalworking and the production of leather and textiles. Just as revealing is that in Dinas Powys, Castle Dore and South Cadbury the remains of a substantial great hall was discovered, a sure indication that all three sites were seats of power during this period. By contrast no such remains were found at Castell Degannwy, but the amount of imported pottery elevate the site to the same status as a royal seat of power.

Other important sites are suggested in the written records. For instance, the *Anglo-Saxon Chronicle* records that at the Battle of Dyrham (AD 577) three British *cyninges* (sub-kings) were slain, the rulers of the former Roman towns of Cirencester (Corinium), Gloucester (Glevum) and Bath (Aquae Sulis). Archaeology has shown that all three towns maintained some form of garrison during the 4th century AD, particularly Glevum, which contained a substantial Roman fort within its walls. It is likely that these *civitates* developed into political units in their own

A reconstruction of a Romano-British warlord, based on archaeological evidence. This is roughly how the defenders of South Cadbury, Dinas Emrys or Tintagel might have looked. Drawing by David Lloyd Owen. (Camelot Research Committee)

right, and continued to maintain their own civil militias until the disaster at Dyrham. As a result of the battle the Saxons managed to cut post-Roman Britain in two, and thereafter the link between Dumnonia to the south and the British lands in Wales and the north could only be maintained by sea. The important fact here is that it seems that until the late 6th century these cities could maintain a field army, and were jointly seen as a political power.

These royal fortifications were also places where annual tribute could be brought, troop musters held and law courts convened. The Welsh annals talk of elaborate systems of food rent and obligatory military service, both of which would be needed in time of war. Therefore, these royal seats of power would also have contained substantial granaries and barrack rooms, designed to be used at set periods, usually between the times of planting and harvesting. In later centuries royal courts tended to be peripatetic, touring from town to town, collecting food rent as they went. However, the Welsh documentary evidence suggests the royal courts of Late Antiquity were static, visited up to six times a year by subjects who owed tribute. The 10th-century Laws of Hywel Da also mentioned plunder as a source of revenue – whether gained from raiding or from the spoils of the battlefield. It stated that the British king took a third, while his body-guard took a share with its commander receiving a double-sized portion of loot. Such divisions would almost certainly be made in the safety of the royal fortress stronghold.

We also know a little about what form this tribute probably took. Animal bones were found during the excavation of many of these forts, mainly of domestic animals such as cattle, pigs and sheep. It seems that the occupants of the fort at Dinas Powys were particularly keen on pork. Shellfish was evidently eaten in coastal forts, while surprisingly few sites produced evidence of game consumption – boar, stag or birds. Of course these domestic cattle could also produce milk, butter and cheese, and the raw materials for several domestic industries. Stock raising was widely practised by both Britons and Saxons, while arable farming was less commonplace.

Of course this was also a heroic warlike society, and kings were meant to be military leaders as well as just rulers of a realm. The *Anglo-Saxon Chronicle* is filled with the exploits of Saxon war leaders – kings or *ealdormen* (co-rulers) who fought against the Britons during the 5th and 6th centuries. Saxon poems and legends such as *Beowulf* or British verse like *Y Gododdin* place great importance on the status of the warrior king, on battlefield heroism and in martial achievements. However, kings didn't always command armies – the *Anglo-Saxon Chronicle* cites several cases where lesser warlords assumed command. The Laws of Hywel Da specify that these men – often the commander of the royal bodyguard – should be the son of the king, or his nephew.

This ivory carving of a Roman general at Monza Cathedral, near Milan, is generally assumed to represent Stilicho, who campaigned in Italy and the Balkans. However, his appearance would be similar to the leaders of Romano-British armies during the 5th century AD. (Stratford Archive)

BELOW
This reconstruction of a Saxon chieftain of the 7th century AD draws heavily on finds recovered from the Sutton Hoo ship burial. His is therefore shown wearing 'ceremonial armour' which is almost Roman in appearance. Drawing by David Lloyd Owen. (Camelot Research Committee)

This was a highly stratified warrior society, so these warlords would probably have their own bodyguard, be they Romano-British *comitates* ('followers') or Saxon *heord-geneatas* ('hearth companions'). These royal and warlord bodyguards were permanent forces, based in the stronghold of their leader and maintained throughout the winter at his expense. This is exactly what the great halls at South Cadbury, Castle Dore, Birdoswald and elsewhere were for – places where these warriors could gather around their leader during the long months of winter, feasting, telling tales, and preparing for the start of a new campaign.

One final aspect of some of these fortified sites was religious importance. We know that some important forts of Late Antiquity, such as Bamburgh or Tintagel, included a chapel within their perimeter, and we can assume that other important sites followed their lead. In return for royal patronage the priest would presumably offer prayers for the ruler and his army. Of course this had its disadvantages – it is claimed that when the Saxon king Aethelfrith of Northumbria found monks praying on behalf of his British opponents at the Battle of Chester (AD 615) he ordered them to be captured and executed. The archaeologist Francis Pryor makes the point that following the collapse of Roman secular authority in the early 5th century AD the existing Christian church offered a degree of continuity and authority in post-Roman Britain, and rulers who embraced Christianity would therefore benefit from a long-established clerical administration as well as being seen as being protectors of Roman culture.

The British and Saxon fortresses of Late Antiquity were therefore far more than just military bastions, although exactly what the role of each site was will probably never be properly understood. Many served as the seats of royal power, and therefore attracted a steady flow of tradesmen, merchants, clerics and tribute-payers. Lesser fortresses served sub-kings or warlords in much the same way, while in a few demonstrable cases the remains of roman towns still maintained their function as a regional marketplace, and as a defensible site in time of war. One of the most important lessons provided by archaeologists is that in most cases these fortified sites maintained links with the wider world, as demonstrated by the presence of imported goods. They also served as a base for professional warriors, and therefore these sites played a pivotal role in the struggle for control of Britain. It is easy to see this military function as being paramount, but without the infrastructure of tribute, taxation and production that underpinned it, these fortresses and the warrior society they served would have been almost impossible to sustain.

FORTS AND WARFARE IN THE 'ARTHURIAN' AGE

The principles of defence

Despite the range of different fortified sites in use in Britain during this period, the limited military options available to both attackers and defenders meant that the principles involved in positional warfare did not vary much. In fact, many of the basic principles of defence are the same as those discussed in *The Forts of Celtic Britain* (Osprey Fortress Series 50). In its most basic form the 'Arthurian' hill-fort worked as a defensive position in much the same way as an Iron Age one: an inner perimeter was encircled by a wooden palisade, which in turn was ringed by banks or ditches. Access to the fort was through a fortified gateway, and in many cases the whole fort took advantage of the terrain to augment its defensive qualities.

Of course, there were differences. The most obvious was in the scale of the fort itself. With the exception of South Cadbury, whose defences enclosed an area of some 18 acres (7.3 hectares), all of the forts of Late Antiquity were far smaller than the typical hill-forts of the Iron Age. The majority of these later forts are less than a fifth of the size of South Cadbury, enclosing an area less than 4 acres (1.6 hectares). Many are much smaller, including some sites which may have been of considerable importance during this period, such as Castle Dore in Cornwall and Dinas Powys in South Wales. One of the largest is Cadbury–Congresbury in Somerset, whose defensive perimeter encloses an area of some 8.5 acres (3.4 hectares). However, these defences were

In the 6th century AD this entrance into the circular inner perimeter of Castle Dore in Cornwall was almost certainly the site of an 'Arthurian' gatehouse. This Iron Age site was refortified during Late Antiquity, and has been associated with the semi-mythical figure of King Mark of Kernow, or Cornwall. (Steve Beckwith)

Castle Dore in Cornwall is a circular Iron Age fortification which was reoccupied and refortified during Late Antiquity. The remains of a large 'Arthurian' hall have been discovered within its defensive banks. (RHAHM)

constructed in the Iron Age, before the coming of the Romans. When the site was reoccupied in the 5th century AD only half of the hilltop was enclosed by a new defensive work. An even more spectacular example is provided by Garn Boduan in Gwynedd, where the later 5th-century fort occupied a small corner of the earlier Iron Age hill-fort. The difference in size has been attributed to the way the armies of Late Antiquity were organized.

The *Anglo-Saxon Chronicle* is the only source which suggests post-Roman British armies were fairly substantial, mentioning forces of 2,000 to 5,000 men. However, at its height the Roman Army in Britain mustered just 6,000 men, so these figures are highly unlikely – possibly little more than poetic propaganda. Professor Alcock argued that the 7th-century Laws of Ine of Wessex stated that a group of three dozen men or more constituted an 'army', and cited the example of Saxon raiding parties listed in the *Anglo-Saxon Chronicle* to justify a much smaller size of force. In AD 449 the Saxon leaders Hengist and Horsa arrived in Britain with three ships, while a similar-sized force was used by King Aelle in AD 477. In AD 495 Cedric and Cynric commanded five ships, while in AD 501 the Saxons Port, Bieda and Maegla raided in two vessels. In the late 19th century the remains of a Saxon oared 'longship' dating from the late 4th century AD was discovered close to the German–Danish border. It was 75ft (23m) long, and had oar benches for around 50 men. Many more occupants would have made the vessel too overcrowded for even the briefest of cross-channel voyages. Therefore we have a more accurate idea of army size than that provided in the *Chronicles*. The Saxon armies which operated in 5th-century Britain mustered no more than 100–250 men.

This ties in neatly with the 300-man force mentioned in the Welsh heroic poem *Y Gododdin*, which supposedly marched south from Din Eiden (Edinburgh), and which was wiped out in battle against the Saxons from Deira at the Battle of Catraeth (Catterick) in *c.* AD 600. Another version uses the symbolism of the number three, claiming the army was 'three hundred, three score and three' (363 men). This is perhaps a far more realistic size for an army of the period than the *Chronicle* figures, and suggests why the

The banks at Ambresbury in Essex are still over 10ft (3m) high in places, and archaeological evidence suggests that the site was briefly reoccupied in the 5th and early 6th centuries AD. This small fort was well placed to act as a buffer against Saxon expansion from East Anglia towards London and the Thames Valley. (Nick Salmon)

fortifications of Late Antiquity were far smaller than those of the Iron Age. Fortified sites like Dinas Powys, Dinas Emrys, Castle Dore and Garn Boduan were little more than fortified halls – the defensive works created to protect the seat of power of a local ruler. Consequently these sites would have been defended by no more than a few hundred men – far too few to adequately defend the perimeter of most of the older Iron Age hill-forts.

Professor Alcock describes many of these small forts as being 'defended homesteads', or even 'enclosed hut groups', and he likens them to the brochs found in northern Scotland – a refuge against a hostile raiding party, or sometimes the fortified stronghold of a local ruler. This hardly fits into the 'Arthurian' myth of an organized post-Roman British resistance to the Saxons, or to the maintenance of field armies capable of strategic offensive operations. As such the business of defending these sites was relatively straightforward. When faced with the possibility of attack the defenders would line the palisade, concentrating their forces at any gatehouse, which was probably considered the most vulnerable area. At Castle Dore and Dinas Powys this palisade was probably wooden, but sat on top of a dry-stone base, much like the inner wall described in our tour of South Cadbury–Camelot. In other cases – Dinas Emrys and possibly at Garn Boduan – this perimeter was built either entirely or largely from stone, using techniques first seen in some of the Iron Age hill-forts of Wales, such as Tre'r Ceiri.

The palisade itself was preceded by a ditch, and this, added to the stone-fronted bank of the inner defensive wall and palisade would have been

F **NEXT PAGE: THE 'ARTHURIAN' GATEWAY: THE MAIN GATEHOUSE, SOUTH CADBURY, WILTSHIRE**

The archaeological evidence for the south-eastern gateway into the South Cadbury hill-fort was slight – little more than the remains of postholes, traces of a roadway and a scatter of stonework. However, this was enough to build up a reasonable picture of the structure, based on known late Roman examples from elsewhere in Europe. The postholes suggested a square structure, spanning the whole width of the 12ft (3.5m)-wide roadway, creating what was essentially a rectangular wooden box. The front of the gatehouse was fitted with a pair of hinged double doors, with a 10ft (3m) span, and which opened inwards. A matching set at the rear of the box opened outwards onto the interior of the fort.

The rest of course is pure speculation. We know it was a reasonably substantial structure, and archaeologists have suggested it contained both an upper chamber above the gateway itself, and a lookout platform on top of the whole structure. These would have been wooden, or possibly constructed from wattle and daub, and would have had a distinctly Roman appearance. The gatehouse itself was flanked by the inner defensive ramparts of the fort, set on top of a stone-filled and timber-latticed bank.

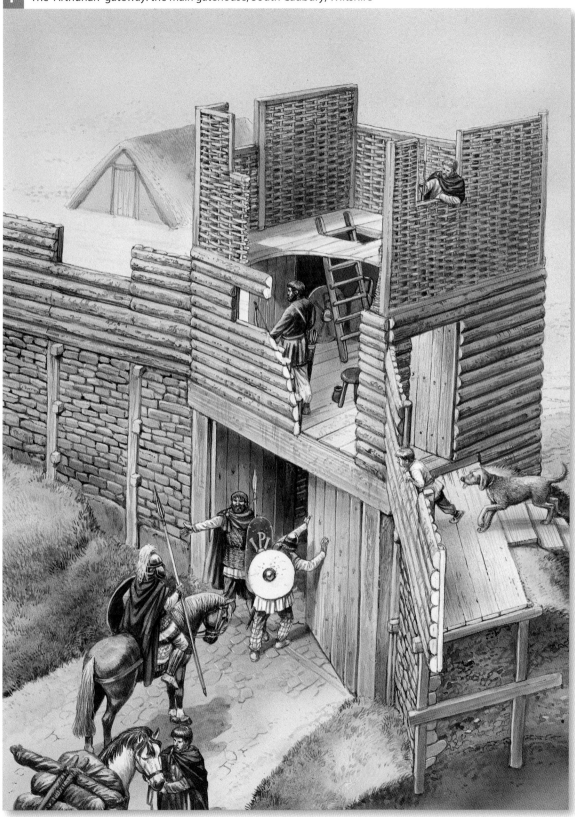

Sites in the war fought between the Britons and the Saxons

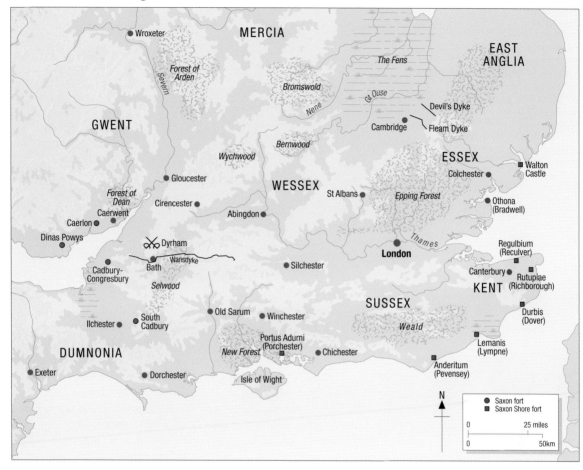

a real obstacle to any attacker. In order to climb the palisade and enter the fort an assailant would need help in the form of either a ladder or siege equipment. As the use of military engineering and siege warfare techniques seem to have been lost when the professional Roman army departed from Britain, the options open to any attacker would have been extremely limited. That left the gate tower, which by necessity had to be approached by a road, or at least a pathway. In sites where access was controlled by geography the terrain would play into the hands of the defender. For instance, at Bamburgh the hilltop plateau was surrounded by a steep crag, and the interior of the fort was accessed through a fortified cleft in the crag.

At Dinas Emrys the approach route wound its way up the more accessible western side of the crag, passing through two defended gateways before reaching the fort interior. An assaulting force would have to storm these outer works before tackling the main perimeter of the fort, and all the while they would be exposed to missile fire from the top of the crag above them. In these circumstances any assault would be a daunting prospect. The secondary approach to Dinas Emrys was along a path that ran along the spine of a narrow ridge, meaning that attackers would have to approach the defences in single file. Once they reached the plateau the path ran below the stone walls of the north-eastern corner of the fort, and again any attacker would have to run the gauntlet of missile fire as they were funnelled beneath the walls.

The key areas involved in the war fought between the Britons and the Saxons in what is now Southern England and Wales during the 'Arthurian' period.

The defences of the Roman city and legionary fortress of Eboracum (York) were extensively rebuilt in the early 4th century AD, and would have still presented attackers with a formidable obstacle in the centuries that followed. In this photograph the base of the Multiangular Tower – part of the city's western defences – is Late Roman, while the upper portion is a medieval addition. (Stratford Archive)

Sites with less clearly defined defensive advantages were still reasonably secure. At Castle Dore in Cornwall the circular perimeter of palisade, bank and ditch was surrounded by an older Iron Age bank and ditch, and although this probably was not fortified, it would certainly delay and hinder an assault party. Another even smaller circular fort at Chun in Cornwall also had an outer circuit of older banks and ditches, while the gatehouse itself was recessed slightly behind the perimeter, and was further protected by flanking spurs which meant that attackers didn't have a clear approach to the gate itself, but would have to pass through a narrow passage – a man-made killing ground immediately in front of the gate. It seems that even the smallest of forts during this period provided adequate enough defences to deter all but the largest group of raiders, and given the rudimentary siege techniques of the time they would have offered a significant obstacle to a larger army.

The *Anglo-Saxon Chronicle* and other Saxon sources contain passing references to the defences of other sites, including larger Iron Age hill-forts such as Old Sarum or Calleva (Silchester) in Hampshire, and Amesbury in Wiltshire. Others, such as Dunum (Hod Hill) in Wiltshire, show signs of having briefly been occupied during Late Antiquity. Given the size of most armies of the time, these positions would have been almost indefensible. If they were fully refortified they would all have required a force of at least 1,000 warriors to properly defend the perimeters, and (with one possible exception discussed later) post-Roman British armies were never this large.

It seems more likely that these sites were used in a similar manner to the Roman marching forts of an earlier age, providing a degree of security to a force when on campaign. All the forts mentioned above were sited in areas which were close to the borders of the Saxons of Wessex, who dominated the Thames Valley from the mid 6th century on, and therefore they would have been well placed to provide protection to passing raiding parties or armies of either side. In the next chapter we shall look at the strategic importance of these and other forts, but for the purposes of studying their defensive properties we can assume that these were negligible. The silted remains of these older Iron Age earthworks would have offered little protection to a defending force, and would have provided nothing more than a slight advantage when fighting a defensive battle.

To some extent the same could be said of the defences of Roman towns, even those which had once been legionary fortresses. The reason was the same as for the older hill-forts: the perimeters of these sites were simply too large to be adequately defended by the small armies available to the rulers and field commanders of Late Antiquity. Even the impressive stone walls of the larger urban fortresses such as Londinium (London) or Eboracum (York) were too large to be adequately defended, unless armed but untrained townspeople were pressed into service. Even that would be a temporary stopgap, and probably inadequate to protect the city walls from being scaled by a determined and well-trained attacking force.

Smaller Roman towns probably had only the most rudimentary defences, as after all, until the early 5th century AD they were all considered safely inside the borders of Britannia, where protection was provided by a highly professional Roman field army. The defences of towns would have been left in the hands of local militias, organized by the *civitates*, and what town wall existed would probably have been wooden rather than stone, designed more to deter felons and wild animals, or to force market goers to pass through toll gates, rather than to stop determined attackers. That said, the three towns of Cirencester (Corinium), Gloucester (Glevum) and Bath (Aquae Sulis) do seem to have maintained their own *civitates* forces, and consequently the towns probably strengthened their own urban defences. Certainly the town defences of Wroxeter were rebuilt in the 6th century AD, and part of the circuit of the older Roman walls was abandoned in favour of a smaller and more manageable perimeter.

Finally we need to take a brief look at the hill-fort of South Cadbury–Camelot, which was clearly in a defensive class all of its own. The old Iron Age hill-fort had been neglected for centuries, but in the late 5th century AD it was reoccupied, and new and extensive defences were erected. The walls were formidable in their own right, particularly as they took advantage of the steep slope of the hill to enhance their qualities as an obstacle. Two or sometimes three outer rings of banks and ditches still remained – relics of the Iron Age fort. In the innermost of these outer rings – the circuit closest to the 5th-century AD defensive perimeter – the ditch showed traces of having been excavated, as the overburden of silt had been removed. The outer ditches appear to have remained untouched.

This shows that the defenders saw these as minor obstacles, of little tactical importance, which would serve to slow or break up an enemy assault up the hill. All the time the defenders could harass the attackers with missile fire. It has even been suggested that while the hill itself would have been cleared of undergrowth, these ditches were allowed to become overgrown, creating a natural barrier of gorse bushes and brambles, without blocking the defenders' field of fire. Once past these outer barriers the attackers would have to storm the wall itself, which was preceded by a wide ditch. The palisade itself was set on top of a dry-stone base, elevating it

The hill-fort of South Cadbury in Somerset was surrounded by a series of banks and ditches, all but the innermost of which date from the Iron Age. This view shows the innermost bank and ditch – the phase associated with the 'Arthurian' occupation of the hill-fort. (Steve Beckwith)

The Roman fort of Birdoswald on Hadrian's Wall was reoccupied in the late 5th or early 6th century, and a timber hall was built on the ruins of one of two Roman granaries. The upright posts in this photograph mark the location of the hall, while in the background are the ruins of the fort's western gateway. (Stratford Archive)

sufficiently to present the attacker with a formidable obstacle. Then there were the gate towers, which we have already seen were as formidable as anything found on Hadrian's Wall, built only from wood rather than stone.

Like other large Iron Age hill-forts it has been estimated that it needed approximately 800–1,000 men to adequately defend its perimeter. While this is normally much larger than the usual army of Late Antiquity, historians have suggested that the 'Arthurian' host which participated in the Battle of Badon (*c.* AD 500), and which defended Dumnonia from the Saxons of Wessex and Mercia, could well have been this large – the confederation of several princes, the army of a high king, or the force of an 'Arthurian' war leader. Whoever used South Cadbury–Camelot as their base, they were a force to be reckoned with in the decades surrounding the Badon battle, and the hill-fort was probably refortified purely to serve the needs of this important but unknown warlord.

The 'Arthurian' forts in operation

While the historical sources provide us with scant information about the way the forts of Late Antiquity Britain were built and operated, they are a little more forthcoming about the role these forts played in warfare during this period. Still, there are significant gaps in our knowledge, both of the part played by the forts themselves, and also the way battles were fought, where they took place, and even who campaigned in which area. Nennius's 8th-century *Historia Brittonum* provides us with a list of battles, supposedly fought by Arthur:

> Then Arthur fought against them in those days, with the kings of the Britons, but he himself was the leader in the battles. The first battle was towards the mouth of the river which is called Glein. The second and third and fourth and fifth were on another river, which is called Dubglas and is in the Linnuis region. The sixth battle was on the river which is called Bassas. The seventh battle was in the wood of Celidon, that is Cat Coit Celidon. The eighth battle was in Castellum Guinnon, in which Arthur carried the image of Saint Mary ever Virgin upon his shoulders, and the pagans were put to flight on that day and there was great slaughter upon them through the virtue of our Lord Jesus Christ and through the virtue of St. Mary the Virgin his Mother. The ninth

battle was waged in the City of the Legion. He waged the tenth battle on the shore of the river which is called Tribuit. The eleventh battle took place on the hill which is called Agned. The twelfth battle was on the hill of Badon, in which 960 men fell in one day in one charge by Arthur. And no-one laid them low save he himself. And in all these battles he emerged the victor.

Much has been written about this entry, and the debate still rages over its reliability, or the existence of the battles it mentions. This, the earliest record of the deeds of Arthur has also been cross-examined by 'Arthurian' believers and sceptics alike. However, our intention is not to prove or disprove the existence of historical figures, but to shed some light on the way fortifications were used in Britain during the wars of Late Antiquity. The importance of this battle list is that it reveals a little about the way wars were fought. The landscape of Britain was different then, with large areas of woodland and occasional swampy areas creating 'no-go' areas for armies, and funnelling them into certain routes. For instance, the New Forest and the Weald effectively protected the Saxon enclaves on the south-east coast of Sussex, while the fenland of East Anglia and the mass of Epping forest to the south helped to protect the Saxons on the eastern seaboard. Selwood ran southwards from Aquae Sulis (Bath) through Dumnonia, creating a protective belt whose southern end was protected by the hill-fort of South Cadbury–Camelot.

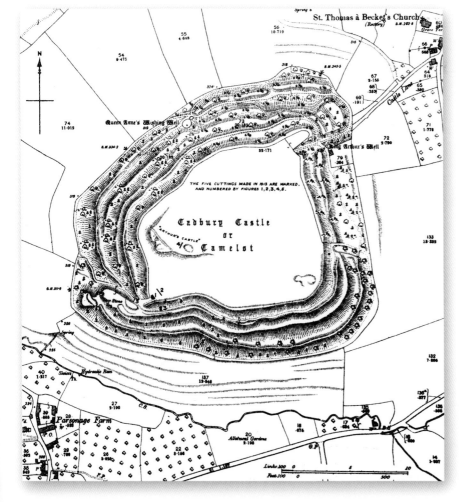

South Cadbury hill-fort, as shown in an Ordnance Survey map dated 1936. This shows the location of the first controlled excavation of the site, conducted in 1915. (Stratford Archive)

47

The Wansdyke at Easton Down, north of Devizes, viewed from the east. The Saxon side of this barrier was on the northern, or left side of this aerial photo. (RCAM)

Armies moved along river valleys, or along the crumbling remains of the old Roman road network. All this meant that terrain played a part in limiting the scope of operations, and consequently towns, river crossings and fortifications all created what a modern soldier would call 'choke points'. Of the battles listed by Nennius, seven were fought on the banks of rivers. The importance of rivers is further underlined by the *Anglo-Saxon Chronicle*, in which numerous battles during this period are described as being fought at a ford. For instance, in AD 571 'Cuthwulf fought against the Britons at Bedcanford, and took four settlements; Limbury and Aylesbury, Benson and Eynsham.' Although we don't know the location of Bedcanford, but given the location of the settlements it was probably a crossing of the River Thames.

Surprisingly Nennius's list contains few sites which could clearly be identified as fortifications. The two places which could host a battle described as being *in urbe Legionis* ('in the City of the Legions') are Caerlon and Chester. Consequently both have been put forward as the site of this battle, which presumably involved a Saxon attack on a British-held Roman fortification. In the Welsh annals, Chester is called 'Gueith cair legion', while Caerlon is called 'Cair Legion guar Usc'. In all honesty the battle could have been fought in either place, despite the numerous books citing the supremacy of one location over the other. For our purposes the more important fact is that the battle almost certainly played itself out beneath the crumbling walls of an old Roman legionary fortress.

Castellum Guinnon, which was listed as the site of Arthur's eighth battle is just as intriguing, as *castellum* suggests a Roman auxiliary fort – a *castella* like Birdoswald on Hadrian's Wall. A case has been made for it being the former Roman fort of Vinovium (Binchester), now in County Durham, although the name Guinnon has never been linked to any known historical figure. The eleventh battle was fought on a hill called Agned, so it may have involved a hill-fort of some kind. The medieval romantic chronicler Geoffrey of Monmouth identified Agned with Dun Eiden (Edinburgh), but this seems to be a purely arbitrary choice. Another version of Nennius names the hill or mountain as Cat Breguoin, which may offer a clue, as the name has been tenuously linked to the Cat gellawr Brewyn mentioned in a poem describing the exploits of King Urien of Rheged.

Brewyn or Breguoin may well have been derived from the Romano-British place name Bremenium, which was a Roman auxiliary fort in the Cheviot Hills of Northumberland near High Rochester. This small multivallate fort covered 4.5 acres (1.8 hectares), and the remains of its towered gateway still stand. The trouble with linking the battle with the fort is geographical – it lies north of Hadrian's Wall. This places it close to Cat Coit Celidon, one of the few battlefields on Nennius's list which can be identified with any degree of certainty. Most scholars agree it referred to the Caledonian Wood, which covered much of what is now the Scottish Borders. Of course, the location of

Agned is as speculative as almost everything else in Nennius's list. For instance, if we believe the suggested locations, then Arthur fought battles across the length of Britain, from the Scottish Borders down to the English Channel. While armies did make long 'strategic' marches, this still seems excessive.

Various versions of Gildas's *De Excidio et Conquestu Britanniae* describe the battle fought on the hill at Badon as being a siege, or else an engagement which lasted for three nights. This would be in keeping with one army (presumably the British one) taking up a defensive position on a hill, possibly within the defences of an old Iron Age hill-fort, and the Saxons trying unsuccessfully to entice them down from their position. When the British finally did counter-attack, Nennius suggests that under the leadership of Arthur they completely vanquished their foes. This spectacular victory was meant to have stopped Saxon expansion in its tracks,

Even when shrouded in sea mist, Bamburgh Castle still dominates the Northumbrian coast. In the 7th century AD the crag on which the medieval castle now stands was occupied by an Anglo-Saxon fortress, the seat of the Kings of Northumbria. (Stratford Archive)

buying almost half a century of relative peace in the process. The term relative is important, as Gildas suggests that the Britons still fought amongst themselves, and no doubt British and Saxon raiding parties still crossed the frontiers into enemy territory on occasion.

The *Anglo-Saxon Chronicle* tells us that the old Iron Age hill-forts of Old Sarum in Wiltshire (known as Searoburh to the Saxons), or Barbury Castle in Wiltshire (referred to as Beranbyrig, or Bera's Stronghold), were the scene of battles fought between the Saxon army of Cynric and Ceawlin in AD 552 and 556. Unfortunately the terse statements in the *Chronicle* tell us nothing more. Archaeology has shown that neither fort was refortified in the

Brent Ditch in Cambridgeshire is the southernmost of the three major Anglo-Saxon earthworks designed to protect their East Anglian territories. Today little remains of the 6th-century ditch and bank. (Sam Marks)

G

THE SAXON FORTRESS: BAMBURGH (BEBBANBURGH), NORTHUMBRIA

Bamburgh was a British settlement long before the coming of the Saxons – traces of Iron Age activity have been detected on the craggy plateau on which the medieval castle now stands. In the 6th century AD this site was known as Din Guyardi, and probably served as the stronghold of a local British ruler. The *Anglo-Saxon Chronicle* entry for AD 547 claims that in that year the Ida, King of the Angles established a fortress at Bamburgh, 'which was first enclosed by a stockade, and thereafter by a wall'. In fact by that time the Angles had been occupying the area for the best part of a generation.

Archaeological excavations and geophysical surveys at Bamburgh have revealed the possible location of these 6th

century AD defences, and of the settlement which grew up there around the Northumbrian royal court. It is believed that the earliest gateway onto the summit of the crag was through a cleft in the rock on the north-western side of the plateau. This site – now known as St. Oswald's Gate – was probably protected by an outer work, which followed the course of a similar medieval feature. The inset shows a tentative reconstruction of the Late Antiquity gatehouse, which was essentially a guardhouse built over the cleft, which had been widened to permit traffic through this highly-defensible entranceway. Bamburgh remains the only known example of an Anglo-Saxon fortress from this period.

'Arthurian' period, so the suspicion is that like the mysterious Badon they were either used as defensive positions by an outnumbered British army, or that the battle was fought nearby, and simply named after these prominent features of the 6th-century landscape.

Another important entry is that for AD 491: 'Here Aelle and Cissa besieged Anderitim, and killed all who lived there; there was not even one Briton left there.' Then the entry for AD 530 states: 'Here Cerdic and Cynric took the Isle of Wight and killed a few men at Wihtgarresbyrg.' Anderitum was the Saxon Shore fort at Pevensey in Sussex, but again the entry fails to tell us whether the garrison was a military one, or merely a place of apparent refuge for civilians, who tried to escape the marauders within the crumbling walls of the Roman fort. The likely location for Withgar's stronghold is the site of Carisbrooke Castle, in the centre of the Isle of Wight. It has been claimed that the fortress was Wihtgarresbyrg (the stronghold of the inhabitants of Wight). Again, no details of the assault were given, and so the snippet adds little to our caucus of knowledge.

The walls of the 'Saxon Shore' fort of Anderitum (Pevensey), in Sussex. Archaeologists have no firm idea of how these fortresses were used during Late Antiquity, and there is little archaeological evidence to suggest they were garrisoned by the post-Roman British. (Steve Danes)

Another known assault on an old Roman fort is provided by Bede, who describes how King Oswald of Northumbria besieged the British warlord Cadwallon in an un-named fortified town. The British sallied, and Osric and his army were defeated (AD 634). Although this fortified town has never been convincingly identified, the likelihood is that Cadwallon took refuge within

The Saxon fortress: Bamburgh (Bebbanburgh), Northumbria

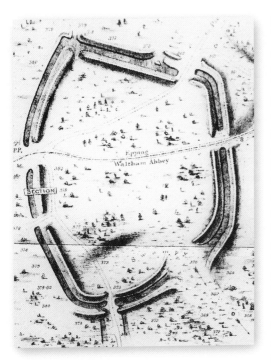

The Iron Age hill-fort of Ambresbury in Essex stands on the northern edge of Epping Forest, and was reputedly an *oppidum* of the Catevellauni tribe during the 1st century AD. It has been suggested that its name was derived from Ambrosius Aurelianus, who first organized resistance against the Saxons in the 5th century AD. (Nick Salmon)

the walls of Eboracum (York). A Welsh source called *The Northern British History* describes how King Urien of Rheged, whose kingdom bordered the west coast of what is now Northern England, besieged King Theodoric 'the Firebrand' of Bernicia on Ynys Metcaut (Lindisfarne) on the east coast for three days and nights (AD 590). Urien's campaigns a decade earlier were centred around Catraeth – formerly the Roman town of Cataractonium – which grew up around an older Roman fort. This was the site of the climactic battle of Gwawrddur, the hero of the heroic Welsh poem *Y Gododdin*, where 'glutted black ravens on the walls of the fort' watched over the slaughter of the hero and the army of Britons from Dun Eiden (Edinburgh) in or around AD 600. Incidentally, the same stanza claims that 'Though he was no Arthur, Among the great ones in the battle, in the front rank, Gwawrddur was a wall.' The Roman fort had been abandoned in the early 5th century AD, but its stone walls were probably still regarded as a formidable defensive position. Archaeological investigation has suggested that the walls of the fort encompassed an area of some 18 acres (7.3 hectares) – making it the same size as South Cadbury–Camelot – and its walls were over 7ft (2.1m) at their base. Evidently this structure was still in reasonable shape almost two centuries after its abandonment. However, British assaults on strongholds of any kind were rare: the doomed assault on Catraeth remains the only example of one in contemporary poetry.

As for Bamburgh itself, the *Anglo-Saxon Chronicle* claims that it was built by King Ida of Bernicia in AD 547, and encircled first by a stockade, and later by a wall. Another version replaces the word 'stockade' with hedge. The old British name for Bamburgh was Din Guyardi or Dinguoaroy, and the new Saxon name was adopted by Ida's grandson King Aethelfrith of Northumbria, who reputedly named the settlement after his wife Bebba – Bebbanburgh around AD 600. During the campaign of AD 590, King Urien's ally King Fiachna of Ulster reputedly captured the Bernician stronghold of Din Guyardi, although not unsurprisingly this claim is not mentioned in the Saxon accounts. The Saxons were no great fort builders, which may explain the rudimentary early protection of Din Guyardi – a hastily built refortification of an existing British promontory-style fort sited on a crag overlooking the sea. However, the site was important as it protected the northern Saxon beachhead in Britain, and as such probably warranted some degree of protection. Bamburgh remains the sole clear example of a Saxon fort of this period.

What these few sources really tell us is that sieges, or at least battles fought around fortifications appear to have been a rarity in the Britain of Late Antiquity. The dearth of references to forts in battle underlines the general assumption that warfare was largely a mobile affair, with raiding parties or small armies striking into enemy territory, where battles were fought more for control of river crossings than for strongpoints or even the remains of towns. Of course this changed – the rapid Saxon expansion of the late 6th and early 7th centuries AD meant that, in order to conquer British land, the attackers had to capture British-held forts. However, when these assaults came it seems that the British preferred to fight for their survival in open battle rather than risk being trapped in a besieged fort. While forts would play a part in these battles, they became prizes of war rather than objectives, the spoils which followed Saxon victory on the battlefield.

AFTERMATH

Gildas wrote his *De Excidio Britanniae* (*On the Ruin of Britain*) as a jeremiad which railed against the current state of post-Roman Britain and the shortcomings of its rulers. He predicted a catastrophe of biblical proportions if what he saw as the feuding and petty-minded British kings failed to settle their differences, and present a united front to the Anglo-Saxons. What is particularly interesting is that he wrote this polemic book around AD 540, when by all accounts the post-Roman British had enjoyed almost four decades of relative peace with the Anglo-Saxons. However, Gildas claimed he could see the writing on the wall.

He was right to be alarmed; for decades it seemed that the British kingdoms had fought amongst themselves, and Gildas cites this internecine feuding and penchant for insurrection and civil war as the great failing of the British. Certainly the Saxons did much the same thing, but the Saxon kingdoms also co-operated with each other on occasion, and for the most part they had the advantage of both organization and numbers. The first phase of Saxon expansion after the Badon peace took place in the AD 550s, when the Saxons from Wessex in the Thames Valley captured Winchester, and consolidated their hold over the area north of the New Forest. This was the campaign which involved the overrunning of Old Sarum and Barbury Castle. A quarrel between the Saxons of Wessex and Kent bought a little more time for the British, but in AD 571 the Saxons struck again, heading north-east to secure the Vale of Evesham. Six years later came the Battle of Dyrham, which led to the Saxon capture of Bath, Cirencester and Gloucester. Dumnonia was now isolated from the British kingdoms to the north.

The *Anglo-Saxon Chronicle* entry for AD 584 states: 'Ceawlin and Cutha fought against the Britons at the place which is named Battle Wood, and Cutha was killed; and Ceawlin took many town and countless war-loot.' This victory secured Saxon control over the region north of the Thames, in what is now Oxfordshire. King Ceawlin of Wessex was defeated by the British somewhere near the Wansdyke in AD 593, and he died the following year. His successor Ceowulf continued to put pressure on the Dumnonians, although he was also engaged in fighting his Welsh and Saxon neighbours at the same time. The Wansdyke had probably been constructed in the mid 6th century, and it marked the boundary between British Dumnonia and Saxon Wessex for almost 100 years – a barrier which was more akin to the Berlin Wall or the Israeli wall around the West Bank than any purely military obstacle.

Archaeologists have shown that South Cadbury remained in use during this period, a strategic bastion which may well have housed the main British field army in Dumnonia. In

The inner face of the ramparts of the refortified 'Arthurian' section of the Iron Age hill-fort of Cadbury–Congresbury, Somerset. This later fort was roughly half the size of the pre-Roman fortification. (Steve Beckwith)

During Late Antiquity the principal entrance to the Saxon stronghold was through a gate built into a cleft in the crag, on the north-western corner of the site. Today the medieval ruins of St. Oswald's Gate mark the site of the 7th-century entrance. (Stratford Archive)

northern and western Britain the kingdoms of Rheged and Gododdin resisted the northwards expansion of the Anglo-Saxon kingdom of Northumbria, while the Welsh kings of Powys, Gwynedd and Gwent occasionally sallied out of their mountain stronghold to do battle for control of the contested lands of the British midlands. The campaigns of King Urien of Rheged in the late 6th century, Gwawrddur around AD 600 and King Cadwallon of Gwynedd in the AD 620s all represent British attempts to turn the Saxon tide. Ultimately all of these campaigns were unsuccessful.

The end came for Dumnonia in the mid 7th century AD. In AD 652 the *Anglo-Saxon Chronicle* mentions that Cenwalh of Wessex fought the British at Bradford (upon Avon), a battle which, rather intriguingly, the medieval chronicler William of Malmesbury lists as taking place at Wirtgernes (Vortigern's fortress). This evidently covered a gap in the Wansdyke, and the Saxons poured into Dumnonia (whose people the *Chronicle* describes as *Wealas*, or Welsh). Six years later the Britons were defeated again at the Battle of Peonnum – probably Penselwood, near Wincanton in Somerset. This time the Britons were completely vanquished, and retreated beyond the River Parrett, some 30 miles (50km) to the west. Penselwood lies just eight miles (13km) east of South Cadbury–Camelot. Unfortunately there is no archaeological evidence to show what part the fort played in these 7th-century campaigns, but it can be assumed that it was abandoned in the aftermath of the defeat at Peonnum.

The Saxons of Wessex had little use for hill-forts, and while the new border between Britons and Saxons remained the River Parrett, the hill-fort fell into disuse. A century later the Saxons forced the Dumnonians back again, establishing a new frontier along what is now the Devon–Somerset border. Then in AD 978 Ethelred the Unready became the new ruler of Wessex, inheriting a realm which was troubled by Viking raids. In AD 1010 he founded a burgh ('fortified town') at Cadanbyrig, the Saxon name for South Cadbury. Consequently the hill-fort enjoyed a new lease of life as a Saxon stronghold, which doubled as a commercial and administrative centre. Cadanbyrig remained in operation for less than two decades, although it survived in some form as a settlement until at least the 13th century.

The retreat of the British was repeated elsewhere in the British Isles, and by the mid 6th century AD the Anglo-Saxon realm extended as far as

Edinburgh to the north, the foothills of the Welsh mountains to the east, and the toe of south-west England. This expansion was far from a smooth, continuous process, but after the failure of the last British counter-attacks and the collapse of Dumnonian resistance the outcome was inevitable. The Saxons lacked the military muscle to penetrate into the Welsh mountains, so fortresses such as Dinas Emrys remained in British hands. Rather than conquer the Welsh, King Offa of Mercia (r. AD 757–96) decided to build his own dyke, which ran along the western borders of Mercia. In effect it was a Saxon version of the Wansdyke, a political statement that the British were now contained within their mountainous refuge. The Anglo-Saxons (or English as they came to be known) maintained this border until the 13th century, when King Edward I launched his conquest of the Welsh kingdoms.

The centuries between the departure of the Roman army from Britain until the Saxon campaigns of consolidation in the mid 7th century AD represented a period when the Celtic inhabitants of post-Roman Britain were on the defensive. They represent a steady erosion of their control of the land, and, however impressive their remains look today, their fortifications failed to stem the Saxon tide. This was a dark and confusing period, where historians and archaeologists often fail to agree on what actually happened, or what the archaeological evidence actually means. The vagaries of both the historical evidence and archaeology mean that we may never be able to build up a complete picture of how post-Roman Britain was defended. We can only hope that some time in the future fresh evidence will be uncovered, and we can learn a little more about the fortifications which dotted the landscape of 'Arthurian' Britain.

Arthur himself remains an enigmatic figure, whose existence is only briefly mentioned by his contemporaries, and whose achievements have been the subject of widespread controversy. We will probably never know the real truth about Arthur – whether he was a historic figure at all, or what he actually accomplished if he was. What remains of those dark days in British history are the grass-covered remains of the strongholds. All we can do now is explore these sites, and imagine what might have gone on within the confines of their walls.

The Roman town of Viroconium (Wroxeter) was all but abandoned in the early 5th century AD, only to be rebuilt a century later as a Romano-British capital. This view shows the remains of the Roman bathhouse, which was replaced by an 'Arthurian' great hall. (Stratford Archive)

THE SITES TODAY

The following selection of British fortifications from Late Antiquity includes sites owned and maintained by national bodies such as English Heritage, Welsh Heritage, or by local authorities. Most of the sites listed are open to the public, and some form of self-guided tour is available to visitors. A few others have been included because the sites are highly visible or important, even though direct access to them is sometimes restricted, often because the site is no longer in good repair, or because it is now in private ownership. Some sites are even supported by a museum either at the site or in a nearby town, where artefacts recovered from the excavation of the site are now displayed.

Finally a handful of national or major regional museums are included in the following list, as they contain artefacts which have either been recovered from the sites of the fortifications mentioned in this book, or which help expand our understanding of the people of post-Roman Britain who built these defensive works. Where appropriate website links have been included.

As this book has limited itself to a discussion of post-Roman British fortifications found in England and Wales, sites and museums in Scotland, the Republic of Ireland and Northern Ireland have been omitted. It is hoped that some day the Irish and Scottish forts of Late Antiquity will be the subject of similar books.

There are hundreds of potential sites around fortified sites throughout Britain, so only a handful of these can be included in the following list. Selection has been made after considering a combination of historic importance, public access and the safety of the visitor.

When viewed from the air the man-made terraces on the sides of Glastonbury Tor are highly visible. Despite claims that this represents a 'spiritual staircase' or defensive rings, they most probably are the remains of agricultural terraces dating from Late Antiquity. (RCAM)

England
Fortified sites
Bamburgh Castle, Northumberland
There is evidence that the seaside crag on which Bamburgh Castle now stands was occupied during the Iron Age. It was also probably occupied during the 6th century AD, when in AD 547 the Anglo-Saxon King Ida established his court there. The site remains the only known Saxon fortification in Britain from this period. Today the remains of this early fort are obscured by the impressive castle erected on the crag during the 14th century AD. Today the castle is owned by the Earl of Northumberland and his family, and the site is open to the public. It is still possible to trace the extent of the Anglo-Saxon royal stronghold, and regular archaeological digs are conducted at Bamburgh throughout the summer. The site is open from March until October.
Websites: www.bamburghcastle.com
www.bamburghresearchproject.co.uk

Birdoswald, Cumbria
One of the Roman forts close to the western end of Hadrian's Wall, the fort was also the location of a thriving *vicus* (civilian settlement) during the period of Roman occupation. It appears that the site remained populated after the departure of the Roman army, although many of the buildings fell into disrepair. In the

5th century AD a large timber hall was built over the site of a Roman granary, and it is postulated that Birdoswald was used as the base for a local Romano-British warlord. Today this well-preserved site is open to the public, and a visitor centre tells the story of all the phases of the fort's occupation. The site is open to the public from April until October.
Websites: www.english-heritage.org.uk/server/show/nav.13613
www.museums.ncl.ac.uk/wallnet/bird

Cadbury–Congresbury, Somerset
Another Iron Age fort in Somerset, this time on the southern outskirts of Bristol, Cadbury–Congresbury was reoccupied at some stage during the 5th century AD. This later fort was concentrated on one side of the plateau, and probably survived until around AD 700. The remains of a large circular building dating from this period can still be found in the centre of the perimeter, near the gates of the 'Arthurian' fort. The site can be reached from a car park, located on the southern end of the nearby village of Yatton.
Website: www.themodernantiquarian.com/site/3848/cadbury_hillfort.html

Castle Dore, Cornwall
This small circular fort dates from the Iron Age, but it was refortified during Late Antiquity, becoming the fortified base for a local king or warlord. Traditionally Castle Dore is associated with the 6th-century King Mark of Kernow (Cornwall), who featured in the romantic legend of Tristan and Isolde. However, no archaeological evidence has firmly tied the ruler to the site. However, during this later period of occupation a great hall was built in the centre of the circular perimeter, which strengthens the supposition that the site served as the seat of an important 'Arthurian' ruler. The site is accessible throughout the year, and is located two miles north of Fowey.

Glastonbury Tor, Somerset
One of the most celebrated sites of Arthurian legend, Glastonbury Tor is a small conical hill which in the 6th century AD rose above the marshy waters of the Somerset Levels. The remains of earthworks dating from the 5th century AD have been found on its summit, which may have been a small fortified homestead, or possibly a pre-Christian religious building. The post-Roman Britons called the tor Ynys Witrin ('Isle of Glass'). Today the site is maintained by the National Trust, and is fully open to the public.
Website: www.glastonburytor.org.uk

Pevensey, Sussex
Probably the largest and best preserved of all the Late-Roman 'Saxon Shore' forts, Anderitum (Pevensey) still remains an impressive fortification, despite later medieval embellishments. During the 6th century AD it was sited at the end of a small peninsula, surrounded by coastal marshland. According to the Anglo-Saxon Chronicle Anderitum was stormed by the Saxons in AD 491, and the British defenders were slaughtered. Today the well-maintained site is run by English Heritage, and is open to visitors throughout the year. A small exhibition on site contains artefacts dating to both the Roman and post-Roman periods of occupation.
Website: www.english-heritage.org.uk/server/show/nav.14191

The circular inner ramparts of Castle Dore in Cornwall were surrounded by a simple ditch, the remains of which can be seen here. It was almost certainly deeper in Late Antiquity, while the bank of the inner ramparts on the left was probably slightly higher, and surmounted by a palisade. (Steve Beckwith)

South Cadbury–Camelot, Somerset

Although this crucially important 'Arthurian' hill-fort was fully excavated during the late 1960s, the site was subsequently returned to its natural state, and hence there are few extant remains for a visitor to see. However, the course of the multivallate defences can still be seen, as can the crest of the hill where the 'Arthurian' great hall once stood. Public paths skirt the perimeter of the hill, allowing visitors to gain an impression of the scale of the Cadbury defences. The site is reached from a car park on the south side of the village of South Cadbury, where a path leads directly to the summit.
Website: www.earlybritishkingdoms.com/archaeology/cadbury.html

Tintagel, Cornwall

Tintagel is probably the most spectacular historic site in the south-west of England – a fort built on an island, which is linked to the mainland by a narrow pathway. The 11th-century chronicler Geoffrey of Monmouth first associated Tintagel with Arthur, and today the site is inescapably linked to the 'Arthurian' legend. During Late Antiquity the site was fortified, and contained both secular buildings – probably the base of a local ruler – and a Celtic monastery. Today only a few traces of these earlier buildings remain, as the mainland part of the site is dominated by the ruins of a 13th-century castle. The site is maintained by English Heritage, and is open to visitors throughout the year. A short distance from the castle is Tintagel Church, a beautiful medieval structure built on the site of an earlier Christian or even pre-Christian religious site.
Websites: www.english-heritage.org.uk/server/show/nav.15393
www.cornwalltour.co.uk/tintagel.html

Although in places the East Wansdyke in Wiltshire still remains an impressive earthwork barrier, its defences have been eroded by centuries of agricultural activity. In this view the dyke is in the middle distance, looking north towards Morgan's Hill. (Marcus Cowper)

Wansdyke, Somerset and Wiltshire

This linear earthwork built in the 5th or 6th century AD stretches from the Iron Age hill-fort of Maes Knoll in Somerset to the Savernake Forest near Marlborough in Wiltshire, some 50 miles (80km) to the east. It was designed as a barrier, dividing the Britons of Dumnonia from the Saxons of Wessex. The earthwork is divided into two main sections – the East and West Wansdyke – and archaeologists are still unsure whether both sections were built at the same time or even by the same people. Most of the Wansdyke is accessible to visitors on foot. The East Wansdyke is better preserved than the West Wansdyke, as it has been less disturbed by agriculture, and in places the bank is over 18ft (4m) high.
Website:
www.wansdyke21.org.uk/wansdykehomepage.htm

Wroxeter, Shropshire

Once a relatively prosperous Roman town, called Viroconium, Wroxeter was largely abandoned during the 5th century AD, only to have its centre rebuilt and refortified in the mid 6th century AD, albeit on a smaller scale. It is believed that Wroxeter was an important fortified regional capital, possibly the seat of the British Kings of Powys during the 'Arthurian' period. After its abandonment around AD 700 the town was never built over, thus presenting archaeologists with a unique resource. Today the remains of the Roman city are preserved by English Heritage, which maintains a visitor centre and museum that interprets the history of both the Roman and the 'Arthurian' town. The site is located five miles east of Shrewsbury, and is open throughout the year.
Websites: www.english-heritage.org.uk/server/show/nav.16832
www.roman-britain.org/places/viroconium.htm

Tintagel in Cornwall is a site that is closely associated with the 'Arthurian' legend, and it contains the remains of both secular and religious structures. This view looking from the mainland towards the island shows the remains of secular buildings on the right of the picture, medieval walls on the left, and the ruins of a Celtic monastery on the summit. (Stratford Archive)

Museums
The British Museum, Great Russell Street, London

The leading historical museum in the British Isles, the British Museum contains a vast collection of artefacts dating from Late Antiquity, the most prestigious of which are the Anglo-Saxon grave finds from the Sutton Hoo ship burial, dating from the early 7th century AD. In addition the museum contains a significant collection of Late Roman, Romano-British and post-Roman British objects. The museum is open throughout the year.
Website: www.britishmuseum.org

Bede's World, Jarrow, Northumbria

This site is more of a historical theme park than a conventional museum, although its new museum facilities are of an extremely high quality, and tell the story of the Anglo-Saxon cleric and scholar, and the Saxon world he inhabited. The site contains reconstructions of several Anglo-Saxon buildings, an Anglo-Saxon demonstrative farm and the site of Bede's monastery of St. Paul's, founded in AD 681. Although these exhibits only contain passing references to the fortifications, weapons and warfare, Bede's World provides an excellent introduction to life in Anglo-Saxon England during Late Antiquity. The site is open throughout the year.
Website: www.bedesworld.co.uk

Like many of the Welsh forts of Late Antiquity, Castell Degannwy near Conwy in Gwynedd takes advantage of a superb natural position to enhance the defensive qualities of the site. During this period the fort was associated with the local ruler Maelgwyn. (RCAMW)

Wales
Fortified sites
Castell Degannwy, Gwynedd
An impressive multi-period site, Castell Degannwy is built on two crags which overlook the mouth of the River Conwy, beside the village of Degannwy, just outside Llandudno. While most of its extant remains are medieval, dating from the early 13th century AD, according to Nennius Castell Degannwy was the stronghold of Maelgwyn, Prince of Anglesey, who died in AD 547. The 6th-century stronghold was located on the western crag, where the ruins of the main castle now stand.
Website: www.castlewales.com/deganwy.html

Dinas Emrys, Gwynedd
Probably the most impressive 'Arthurian' fortification in Wales, Dinas Emrys is sited on a crag overlooking the River Glaslyn valley. While the crag can be climbed, it can be dangerous, and visitors are advised to contact the National Trust for Wales warden at the Craflwyn basecamp, in the nearby village of Beddgelert. It takes an hour to climb the ridge to the north-east corner of the fort; an approach up the western slope is not advisable due to the danger of rock falls.
National Trust Warden: Tel (0176) 651-0120
Websites: www.castlewales.com/dinas_em.html
www.nationaltrust.org.uk/main

Dinas Powys, South Glamorgan
Located beside the village of the same name on the western outskirts of Cardiff, Dinas Powys might be a site that dates back to Late Antiquity, but its original walls were replaced by a stone-built castle in the 11th and 12th centuries AD. Today little trace can be found of the earlier fortification, although the site is still well worth a visit.
Website: www.castlewales.com/dinas_pw.html

Garn Boduan, Gwynedd

Another spectacular hill-fort, Garn Boduan is actually two hill-forts, one located inside the other. The larger fort is an Iron Age site, and contains the remnants of over 170 circular huts within its stone-built perimeter. On its eastern side is a much smaller site, which probably dates to the late 6th century AD. The hill-fort can be reached on foot from the nearby road – details of the brisk hour-long walk are posted on both of the listed websites.
Websites:
www.bbc.co.uk/wales/northwest/sites/celts/pages/garnboduan.shtml
www.rhiw.com/y_pentra/llyn_to_do/llyn_walks/garn_boduan/garn_boduan.htm

Museums
National Museum of Wales, Cathays Park, Cardiff

The displays of this museum include finds dating to Late Antiquity, along with a historical interpretation of the period. Open daily (except Mondays) from 10am to 5pm.
Website: www.museumwales.ac.uk/en/home

BIBLIOGRAPHY

Alcock, Leslie *Arthur's Britain: History and Archaeology, AD 367–634* (London, 1971)

Alcock, Leslie *By Cadbury, is that Camelot...: Excavations at Cadbury Castle, 1966–1970* (London, 1975)

Alcock, Leslie *Economy, Society and Warfare among the Britons and Saxons* (Cardiff, 1987)

Anderson, Perry *Passages from Late Antiquity to Feudalism* (New York, 1978)

Ashe, Geoffrey *A Guidebook to Arthurian Britain* (London, 1980)

Bédoyère, Guy de la *Eagles over Britannia* (Stroud, 2001)

Brown, Peter *The World of Late Antiquity* (London, 1971)

Carver, Martin (ed.) *The Age of Sutton Hoo: the Seventh Century in North-Western Europe* (Rochester, NY, 1999)

Charles-Edwards, Thomas *After Rome* (Short Oxford History of the British Isles series, Oxford, 2003)

Davies, Wendy *Patterns of Power in Early Wales* (Oxford, 1990)

Fields, Nic *Rome's Saxon Shore* (Osprey Fortress series No. 56, Oxford, 2006)

Frere, Sheppard *Britannia: A History of Roman Britain* (Trowbridge, 1967)

Gidlow, Christopher *The Reign of Arthur: From History to Legend* (Stroud, 2004)

Hill, David *An Atlas of Anglo-Saxon England* (Oxford, 1981)

Hindley, Geoffrey *A Brief History of the Anglo-Saxons: The Beginnings of the English Nation* (London, 2006)

Hogg, A.H.A. *Hill-Forts of Britain* (London, 1975)

Holmes, Michael *King Arthur: A Military History* (London, 1996)

Johnson, Stephen *Later Roman Britain* (London, 1980)

Konstam, Angus *The Forts of Celtic Britain* (Osprey Fortress series No. 50, Oxford 2006)

McClure, Judith and Collins, Roger *Bede's Ecclesiastical History of the English People* (Oxford, 1994)

Moffat, Alistair *Arthur and the Lost Kingdoms* (London, 1999)

Morris, John *The Age of Arthur: A History of the British Isles from 350 to 650* (London, 1973)

Morris, John (ed. and trans.) *Nennius: British History and the Welsh Annals* (Chichester, 1980)

Pryor, Francis *Britain AD: A Quest for Arthur, England and the Anglo-Saxons* (London, 2005)

Stenton, Sir Frank *Anglo-Saxon England* (London, 1971)

Swanton, Michael (ed.) *The Anglo-Saxon Chronicles* (London, 1973 and 1976)

Thomas, Charles *Britain and Ireland in Early Christian Times* (London, 1971)

Wallace-Hadrill, John Michael *Bede's Ecclesiastical Commentary on the English People: A Historical Commentary* (Oxford, 1998)

Whitelock, Dorothy (ed.) *English Historical Documents I* (London, 1979)

Wilson, David *The Anglo-Saxons* (London, 1960)

Wilson, David *The Archaeology of Anglo-Saxon England* (London, 1976)

Winterbottom, M. (trans.) *Gildas: The Ruin of Britain and Other Documents* (London, 1978)

Wood, Michael *In Search of the Dark Ages* (London, 1981)

Young, Simon *AD 500: A Journey through the Dark Isles of Britain and Ireland* (London, 2005)

GLOSSARY

Anglo-Saxon   The collective term for the Germanic peoples who settled in Britain from the mid 5th century, including the Angles, the Jutes and the Saxons.

Bank   In terms of hill-forts, these are often associated with ramparts, although more accurately the latter represents the final bank before the inner enclosure. Banks were usually but not always built behind a ditch, from which the soil for the bank was excavated.

Berm   A flat space between the foot of a bank and the start of a ditch.

British   In terms of the Late Antiquity this is the collective term for the Celtic inhabitants of Britain during the Roman and Post Roman periods. It therefore encompasses virtually all the indigenous population of the British Isles.

Contour fort   The technical term for a hill-fort built to take advantage of the contours of a hill. Invariably the shape of the fort follows the contour line, producing an irregular shape to the fortification.

Civitas (pl.) *civitates*   A community of citizens (*civites*). In Late Roman and Post Roman Britain the phrase also referred to a form of regional administration, which roughly equates to the county.

Comitates   A Roman term for companions or followers, usually associated with the personal bodyguard of a military or civic leader.

Counterscarp   The exterior slope or wall of a ditch, which in the case of hill-forts was sometimes revetted using stone or timber.

Dyke   An earthwork bank, designed to mark a boundary rather than to act as a defensible barrier. It was often preceded by a ditch.

Earthwork   An earthen embankment, part of a fortification. In most cases a bank or rampart is classified as an earthwork.

Glacis   The slope extending down from the outer works of a fortification over which an attacker would have to move as he approached the fort.

Hill-fort	A defensive earthwork or stone-built Iron Age or Late Antiquity structure built on an easily defensible position, usually the plateau or summit of a hill.
Iron Age	The period from around 700 BC until the Roman conquest of Britain in AD 43 when the inhabitants of Britain produced and used iron.
Late Antiquity	A term used by modern historians to encompass the period between Classic Antiquity and the Middle Ages. It is generally assumed to begin in the late 3rd century AD, and to continue until the mid 7th century AD.
Multivallate	An Iron Age or Late Antiquity fortification system where the central enclosure is surrounded by more than three sets of banks and associated ditches.
Oppidum	A Roman term for a fortified settlement, usually an Iron Age hill-top position. During Late Antiquity the word was sometimes used in association with the strongholds of British warlords or rulers.
Palisade	A wooden fence of stakes, posts and beams that formed a defensive barrier. In most cases these surmounted the ramparts of a Late Antiquity fort.
post-Roman	A term used in British history to describe the period following the departure of the Roman army from Britain in the early 5th century AD, and the subsequent collapse of Roman administration. The general assumption is that this phase ended with the completion of the Saxon conquest of England in the late 7th century AD.
Promontory fort	An Iron Age fortification built on a headland or promontory, where three sides of the position were protected by the sea or even by rivers, leaving just one side that required protection from man-made defensive works.
Rampart	In terms of hill-forts and other Late Antiquity fortifications, a rampart was the last bank defence before the inner enclosure of the fort. A rampart was often surmounted by a palisade, breastwork or other form of parapet.
Revetment	A timber or stone facing to a bank, ditch counterscarp or rampart, designed to protect it from erosion, or to impart additional strength to the structure.
Saxons	A confederation of Germanic tribes who settled in Britain from the mid 5th century onwards.
Timber-laced	The archaeological term for a bank or rampart of earth or stone that was constructed around a timber frame.
Warlord	A local ruler, whose power rested on military strength. The term is often used in lieu of more concrete evidence concerning the lesser British or Anglo-Saxon rulers of Late Antiquity.

INDEX

Figures in **bold** refer to illustrations.